Grade
Power

Also by Kevin Alderson:
Same-Sex Marriage
Breaking Out
Beyond Coming Out

Grade Power

The Complete Guide to Improving
Your Grades Through Self-Hypnosis

Dr. Kevin Alderson, Ph.D.

INSOMNIAC PRESS

Interior design by Marijke Friesen

Library and Archives Canada Cataloguing in Publication

Alderson, Kevin, 1956-
    Grade power : the complete guide to improving your grades through self-hypnosis / Kevin Alderson.

Includes bibliographical references and index.
ISBN 1-894663-67-5

    1. Autogenic training. 2. Academic achievement. I. Title.

RC499.A8A43 2004   370.15   C2004-903945-8

The publisher gratefully acknowledges the support of the Department of Canadian Heritage through the Book Publishing Industry Development Program.

Printed and bound in Canada

Insomniac Press
192 Spadina Avenue, Suite 403
Toronto, Ontario, Canada, M5T 2C2
www.insomniacpress.com

Table of Contents

Preface

I've always been fascinated by the power of the mind and the human spirit. Whenever I think I understand either power, I end up placing one or the other in a box. The box invariably shatters, and I am left once more in awe of something far bigger than I.

Never underestimate the power of the mind. Never underestimate yourself. Strange, though, how nearly everyone does. But who knows what capabilities lie dormant within you right now?

How does a simple man from humble beginnings become President of the United States? How did Abraham Lincoln do it? How did he garner such incredible respect that he was elected? Yes, he was intelligent. Yes, he became well spoken. But was he *destined* to become President? Something deep within him had to change. What was it?

Mahatma Gandhi of India was another great leader. Despite aggressive acts against Indians by the British in their attempts to maintain control and order, the Mahatma preached his message of peaceful resistance in protest of British rule while personally fasting for long periods. What kept driving him so hard? Why didn't he give up?

Ordinary people can do extraordinary things. There are examples of average individuals who have developed incredible strength when needed. Imagine a loved one trapped underneath a car after the mechanism in a vehicle jack fails and the car collapses. Can you imagine lifting up the back end of the car so that your loved one can escape? Without thinking, you might unwittingly do it, as some other "anything-*but*-Arnold-Schwarzenegger" types have done before.

Can you imagine walking to a hospital miles away suffering from a broken back caused by a car accident, and then discovering that you will be physically incapable of walking again for months, if ever? How can your mind rule your body at times of such trauma?

The movie *Titanic* reminded us of the power of love. The human spirit soars to meet any challenge when it becomes convinced that something is necessary, even if it may lead to death. How can we garner just some of this power, preferably without having to die for it?

You know of people who accomplish many goals simultaneously. They work, they go to school, they exercise, they party, they maintain an intimate relationship, and they have time for their friends. Why aren't they insane with stress? How do they do it?

You might wonder, as I did, whether the power of the mind is something that can be amassed and then directed toward a particular goal. In other words, can we control some of this power, or is it only by happenstance or coincidence that it emerges at all?

When I was seventeen, my friend and I were at the annual exhibition, a festival event complete with amusement park rides and sticky cotton candy. An entertainer was about to begin on stage—the Amazing Vandermede—a stage hypnotist who could purportedly hypnotize someone within minutes. My friend heeded his call, and as he left his seat to saunter to the stage, I had little idea of what I would soon witness. My friend was quiet, reserved, similar to myself. Predictably, I suppose, he was in a deep trance within minutes, falling forward and nearly off his chair when Vandermede said, "Now sleeeeeeeep." I felt myself wanting to respond, needing to shake my head to remain consciousness. I wasn't about to be embarrassed, and I didn't think my friend would have felt differently.

I didn't know my friend could sing. I didn't know he could move like an accomplished dancer. I didn't know he had confidence. I didn't know he wasn't shy. I didn't know he could convincingly act like a Casanova. The strange thing was, *neither did he!* After the performance my friend became "himself" again. I never again heard him sing or act with social poise and confidence. He avoided school dances and retreated into the shyness both he and I knew so well.

Since that day, I was never able to let go of the power of hypnosis. I was fascinated by it and I needed to know more. Books on the topic were hard to come by, and I assumed that they were carefully hidden from most of us, like old crusty manuscripts that revealed the secrets of magic. Hypnosis is not magic, of course, but scientific, and a powerful tool. It is something with the proven ability to access the power of the mind.

I'm still fascinated when I see the transformations that result from hypnosis. Unlike my friend's fleeting experience, *permanent change is possible*, and if suggestions are administered correctly, permanent change is inevitable. *Self-hypnosis* is as potent as anything a hypnotist could do for you.

This book is for you, a student struggling to make life easier. If you learn the lessons in this book well, you will not only excel in school, but you will also succeed in life. *Grade Power* is *life power*—the attitudes, beliefs, and skills you develop in becoming a better student are life skills that are transferable to any situation. Turn the page and find out how this book will help.

Introduction

As a student, I wasn't very interested in learning the most effective study skills, or in finding better ways to manage my time. I don't recommend this undisciplined approach—it caused me unnecessary stress. But during many years I spent working in a community college, I noticed that most students tune out when someone starts talking about these academic skills. Let's face it—it can be boring! This book is different, however, every page is packed with practical methods and helpful suggestions. You will enjoy reading it as much as I enjoyed writing it! (If I'm wrong in your case, let me know by e-mailing me at alderson@ucalgary.ca.) Despite how boring learning about academic skills can be, we know that most students who enter college are academically underprepared for what they are about to face (Moss & Young, 1995).

What differentiates those who succeed in school from those who don't? Part II of this book answers this question in depth, as its importance deserves. Success is a predictable outcome, and it is only somewhat related to having top-notch academic skills.

From the outset, know that the most important answer to the question of how to succeed is found in *belief*—the same kind of belief my friend had when he sang and danced. When the *failure script* is replaced by the *success script*, failure becomes nearly impossible. Why? Because it becomes unacceptable. Our inner scripts, which are the repetitive thoughts and beliefs that define who we are, are post-hypnotic suggestions, and if they dictate you will succeed, then you will succeed. Commonly, however, the inner scripts send a different message, a much more negative one. They say, *you can't, you won't, you shouldn't, you're not deserving, you're not capable*, etcetera. Abraham Lincoln, too, had to believe—he had to believe that becoming President was possible, and he had to believe that he was capable. Otherwise, he would never have tried, by working diligently, to make the possible become probable and the probable become actual. We need to believe strongly in ourselves if we are to become truly successful. Chapter 4 shows you how to develop a strong sense of self.

▶ How Can This Book Help?

Belief alone is not enough for academic success, and students still need to have adequate academic skills, especially for post-secondary education. *But it doesn't have to be as difficult as many people think! Grade Power* is about making school easier and more enjoyable.

In this book, you will learn:

• the most effective conventional methods to help you succeed at school,

• to become familiar and comfortable with self-hypnosis,

• about the four powers of success and applications of self-hypnosis,

• how to use self-hypnosis to become a better student.

Educational psychologists and educators already know a great deal about how to help students succeed in school. Each chapter of this book, starting in Part II, begins with a brief review of the best techniques known in the field of student success. These methods alone have been enough to help mediocre students become outstanding students, sometimes without having to increase their study hours. However, *Grade Power* surpasses the conventional know-how on the topic of student success by transporting you into the world of imagination, relaxation, and creativity—the world of self-hypnosis. In this world, you will learn to enter the most powerful part of your mind—your subconscious. As explained in the next two chapters, accessing the subconscious is the field of *mind technology*. Why work harder when, instead, you can work smarter?

▶ Features of This Book
Major Scripts

There are two major scripts in this book. You will be asked in Chapter 2 to make a recording of these scripts. The scripts are complete hypnosis sessions, but more effective because you will listen to them in your own voice. The scripts for each tape will take approximately twenty minutes to record.

Major Script #1

Major Script #1 is called, "The Basics of Self-Hypnosis," and it serves three purposes:
- relaxation,
- ego-strengthening,
- self-hypnosis conditioning.

First, once you have the script recorded, it becomes a relaxation tape. Many people find listening to a tape helpful in teaching them how to better relax. There are several benefits to simply spending time relaxing, and these are explained in Chapter 2. Second, the script contains suggestions for *ego-strengthening*, which is the technical term for suggestions aimed at improving your self-esteem, self-confidence, self-image, and self-concept. Ego-strengthening helps you feel better about yourself. Some people spend hundreds of dollars in their attempts to improve their self-esteem. Listening to your recorded tape may be just as effective. Third, the script also includes instructions for entering self-hypnosis, a technique I call "The Basic Induction." The more times you listen to your tape, the more these instructions will act as post-hypnotic suggestions. In other words, the more you listen to the tape, the better your response should be when practicing self-hypnosis—that means going into self-hypnosis deeper and faster.

Major Script #2

Major Script #2 is called, "Grade Power: Unlocking the Keys," and it contains suggestions and imagery for all of the important academic areas and personal growth areas. Once recorded, the script becomes a generic student success tape. The topics it addresses are:
- believing in yourself,
- increased passion,
- increased motivation and persistence,
- better balance in life,
- better concentration,

- improved study skills,
- positive study attitudes,
- proper exam preparation,
- reduced exam anxiety,
- overcoming writer's block,
- enhanced career exploration.

As the ideas in this script become deeply implanted in your mind, much of what this book covers will become easier to absorb because you will already be familiar with the topic. The content of Major Script #2 corresponds to the chapter topics in Parts II and III of this book. This structure is intended to help bridge the content of the script with what you read and practice in the book. Instructions for making these tapes are found in Appendix 1.

Conventional Methods Section

This section briefly reviews the best techniques generally used to improve the area covered by the chapter. Use these techniques for optimal performance as a student in addition to the self-hypnosis methods described in the next section.

Self-Hypnosis Applications

Many books on self-hypnosis suggest either one or two approaches. This book offers three:

- verbal suggestions/positive affirmations,
- visual imagery,
- recorded script.

Verbal suggestions are statements you make to yourself just before you enter self-hypnosis, once in self-hypnosis, or both. Positive affirmations are similar, except you use them in a slightly different way. Appendix 6 provides instructions on how to use verbal suggestions and positive affirmations properly.

Visual imagery is the use of our imagination to call up a picture, like we do when we daydream. Appendix 5 provides instructions on the use of visual imagery. Some people find that their hypnotic response is best while listening to a tape with suggestions *and* imagery. A script for this purpose is provided in each chapter, beginning in Chapter 4, which you can tape or digitally record and later listen to while in self-hypnosis. Instructions for this practice are contained in Appendix 1.

Try all three approaches before you decide which you will continue to use. Through your experiments with the approaches you may discover whether you are a visual learner or are more influenced by verbal suggestions. Alternatively, if you find it hard to concentrate on either verbal or visual material, the recorded script may be your best alternative. You might also find that each approach is useful at various times.

Summary
A brief summary is found at the end of each chapter. Only the highlights of each chapter are mentioned, offering a quick method for reviewing the chapter's focus and its usefulness to you.

▶ What's Inside
Grade Power is broken into three sections. Part I is called *Foundations of Power*, which includes Chapters 1 and 2. Together, these chapters provide a thorough review of hypnosis and self-hypnosis. Part II is called *Applying the Four Powers of Success*, which includes Chapters 3 through 7. This section is about developing qualities that successful people in general have mastered. Part III is called *Other Powerful Applications*, which includes Chapters 8 through 12. This section focuses on typical academic concerns, as well as some less common ones as well. The following questions reflect the content of the respective chapters.

• How powerful is the mind, and can hypnosis access it? (see Chapter 1)

• What are the clinical uses of hypnosis today? (see Chapter 1)

• What is self-hypnosis, and how can it help me? What about hypnotic tests? (see Chapter 2)

• How does relaxation differ from self-hypnosis? What are its benefits? (see Chapter 2)

• What are the four powers of success? (see Chapters 3 through 7)

• How do I learn to believe deeply in myself? (see Chapter 4)

• How do I develop more passion for life and for my goals? (see Chapter 5)

• How do I become motivated, and then sustain it? (see Chapter 6)

• Why is maintaining a balanced lifestyle so important? How can I become better balanced? (see Chapter 7)

• How do I become better at concentrating, memorizing, and remembering? (see Chapter 8)

• What is the best way to study? How can I make studying easier? (see Chapter 8)

• How do I reduce or overcome exam anxiety? (see Chapter 9)

• How can I overcome writer's block so I write instead of procrastinating? (see Chapter 10)

• How do I reduce or overcome speech anxiety? (see Chapter 11)

• How can I enhance my career exploration through self-hypnosis? (see Chapter 12)

▶ Summary

This introduction has reviewed the many ways that this book can help you as a student. Combined, the major scripts, the conventional methods used to help students become successful, and the self-hypnosis applications help guarantee your success in school, and in life. This introduction also included a brief look at the content of each chapter. The next chapter lays the first foundation of grade power.

Part I

Foundations of Power

Chapter One

Hypnosis and the Power of Suggestion

Everyone uses suggestion to some extent in everyday life. When you offer a chair silently to someone, and he sits down, you have successfully induced suggestion.

(Ziegenfuss, 1962, p. 505)

Hypnosis is everywhere. It appears in many forms, and most people never realize it has already happened to them. Indeed, it is happening to them right now. You are no exception.

Hypnosis is the influence created by other people who are significant to you in some way, and the influence created by your own experience. It occurs anytime you are *really* listening without being judgmental or critical, or when you are *not* listening, but still hearing. This latter instance creates a subliminal effect. If you were never open to suggestion, a state professionals call *suggestibility*, you could not learn or change.

▶ The Four Forms of Hypnosis

Under what conditions do you become more suggestible? Most people are aware of three such conditions: clinical hypnosis, self-hypnosis, and stage hypnosis. However, there are also forms of hypnosis that occur sponataneously, which I will call *natural hypnosis*. By understanding each of these forms of hypnosis, you will develop a much more clear sense of what hypnosis is and what it isn't.

Natural Hypnosis

You can't escape hypnosis. You are predisposed to suggestibility some of the time, and knowing about this predisposition is an important lesson in the way the mind works. You are more suggestible, compared to the normal waking state, under the following 10 conditions:

- shortly before natural sleep and upon awakening from it,
- when tired or relaxed,
- in a state of total concentration,
- when influenced by effective persuasion,
- when experiencing sleep and sensory deprivation,
- during childhood and adolescence,
- when experiencing emotional crisis disturbance,
- when in shock,
- when under the influence of mind-altering drugs and alcohol,
- in a state of hysteria.

Shortly Before Natural Sleep and Upon Awakening From It

Before you go to sleep your brainwaves slow down. When you are just about asleep, but not quite there, your mind becomes very active. If you are roused at such times, you may be aware that you have either been dreaming or daydreaming vividly. During these moments, your mind becomes more suggestible, both to your own suggestions and to those made by others.

Shortly before fully awakening, your mind also becomes more suggestible. Have you ever had the experience of "getting up on the wrong side of the bed"? If you haven't, I want some of your meds! Nonetheless, this is a good example of how a bad dream or negative thought early in the morning can spoil how you subsequently feel that day.

Tiredness or Relaxation

When you are tired or feel relaxed, the analytical part of your mind also relaxes. Have you noticed it is easier to settle an argument when you and the other person remain calm and relaxed, as compared to tense and angry? This is because you become more suggestible to the other person's perspective.

According to Dr. Genuit (1994), most Native American tribes he studied used rhythmical sounds and movements, like drumming and dancing, to induce altered consciousness, creating relaxed states of intense concentration within the participants of these practices. Modern urban culture adds other sounds and creates the "hypnotic experience" young people experience at a nightclub or rave. Drivers have nearly driven off roads as they became hypnotized by a strobe effect created when sunlight shines between intermittently spaced trees, or after they became confused by the effect of snow blowing at their windshields at night.

Total Concentration

Have you ever read a novel that was so engrossing it brought tears to your eyes, or found that a happy sequence put a smile on your face? Do you remember the last time you laughed hysterically at a movie? Words and images can have this effect on you only when you find something compelling—only then do you become suggestible and, in turn, react emotionally.

Effective Persuasion

Have you ever felt emotionally affected, or trapped, by a persuasive salesperson? Effective salespeople have learned every trick in the book to make you succumb to their allure and, ultimately, to the product they want you to buy. If you leave a sales presentation without buying anything and find yourself feeling like a loser, you have become hypnotized into believing that you need a product. Motivational speakers have the same hypnotizing effect—you leave the presentation feeling pumped and ready for action.

Sleep and Sensory Deprivation

The use of sleep and sensory deprivation are established techniques in brainwashing. The truly unfortunate thing is that these techniques work. If you were kept in some kind of bubble and prevented from experiencing anything with your senses, you might find that your mind would not only becomes extremely imaginative, but it might also become very receptive to new ways of looking at things. An example of this phenomenon is found in the fictional movie *Altered States*.

Childhood and Adolescence

It is a well-established fact that children and adolescents are highly suggestible. Young children are impressionable, and the ideas we give them are accepted uncritically. Adolescents become suggestible to their peers and other important figures as they search for a sense of their own identity. The most powerful hypnosis is that which we call *childrearing*.

Emotional Crisis or Emotional Disturbance

Did you ever wonder how cults recruit their members? You probably think it could never happen to you. If you were suffering an emotional crisis, however, or if you experienced long-standing emotional problems, you might find that there are times when you are desperate for a solution—so much so that you might choose the solution that someone else offered you, despite how insane that solution might seem to your friends and family. Crisis counseling is also effective in helping people to change because people become suggestible when they urgently need answers to their problems.

When in Shock

You enter a minor state of shock when you do not have the resources to cope with a particular source of stress or event in your life. A worse state of shock may affect you in times of extreme crisis, such as when you are seriously injured. Children who are yelled at usually enter a state of shock, and for this reason, many of the negative messages directed at them are internalized, thereby lowering their self-esteem and damaging their self-concepts, sometimes for life.

Mind-Altering Drugs and Alcohol

There is no denying it—alcohol impairs judgment and releases your inhibitions. Subsequently, you become more likely to take chances and act on other people's suggestions, including your own. Drugs like LSD, PCP, and marijuana have also shown themselves to make people more suggestible.

Hysteria

Have you ever wondered how intelligent teenagers and adults came to believe that there were witches in Salem, Massachusetts, in 1692? Why is laughing in a movie theater often contagious? Psychologists use the term *hysteria* to explain this effect. Hysteria can spread when something with powerful effects on the senses occurs and witnesses develop similar ways of thinking, feeling, or responding to it. For example, laughing, crying, and feeling sick can all be contagious under the right circumstances.

Stage Hypnosis

Stage hypnosis is the use of hypnosis for fun and entertainment. Are the participants on stage really under the hypnotist's "spell," and consequently forced to obey him or her? Stage hypnosis has fostered a number of misconceptions about hypnosis because of what we think is occurring on stage. What *really* happens? First, the stage hypnotist asks for a number of volunteers to come forward. The fact that these people volunteer indicates that they want to be part of the performance. They also know that if chosen to remain on stage, they will be expected to entertain the audience. Three types of people find their way to the stage—those who:

- are sincerely interested,

- want to test the hypnotist, and prove that they cannot be "made" to do anything,
- go up on a dare or because they feel pressured by friends.

The only participants who have a chance of remaining on stage are the ones who are sincerely interested in experiencing hypnosis. This is because certain factors are necessary for the induction of a hypnotic state, referred to here as the "five Cs" of hypnosis. These include:

- cooperation,
- consent,
- concentration,
- communication,
- conviction (i.e., trust in the hypnotist and in the process).

Only the sincerely interested will meet the criteria for the five Cs. The best subjects for hypnosis are intelligent, creative, imaginative, and relaxed individuals. Above all else, these people are highly motivated to experience hypnosis and its benefits.

Once the stage performance begins, the participants are given a number of suggestions. They know what is being asked of them, and because they want to take part they feel a desire to act out the suggestions. Be aware that there is a difference between a desire and a compulsion. No one is compelled to do anything while in hypnosis. The hilarity of what occurs on stage is a combination of increased suggestibility and performing (i.e., acting).

Clinical Hypnosis

Clinical hypnosis is the result of a relaxed state of mind and body, along with an increased state of suggestibility. Its purpose is to help people overcome problems, or to make problems more manageable, and to help foster personal growth and development. Like stage hypnosis, the five Cs are necessary preconditions if hypnosis is going to occur. Unlike natural hypnosis and stage hypnosis, clinical hypnosis is almost always conducted with the client or patient relaxed throughout the treatment, and the treatment is usually provided by someone with professional credentials in the fields of psychology, psychiatry, medicine, nursing, dentistry, or clinical social work. There are many uses for clinical hypnosis, and the following lists provide just a few examples:

Psychological Uses
- reduce anxiety, including treatment of phobias
- crime detection
- educational enhancement (e.g., the focus of this book)
- deal with habit disorders (e.g., smoking, nail-biting, weight control)
- performance enhancement (e.g., sports)
- reduce or eliminate the symptoms of psychosomatic disorders (e.g., asthma, headaches, irritable bowel syndrome)
- assist with self-esteem building
- treatment of sexual disorder
- stress management

Dental Uses
- control teeth grinding
- reduce excessive salivation
- manage or eliminate needle phobia
- reduce bleeding
- substitute for local anaesthetics

Medical Uses
- alleviate pain, including analgesia (i.e., absence of pain) and anaesthesia (i.e., absence of sensation)
- treat certain types of warts
- cure bedwetting
- encourage the growth of breasts in females
- treat insomnia
- allow relaxation during childbirth (i.e., natural childbirth)

Self-Hypnosis

Self-hypnosis is also a relaxed state of increased suggestibility, but you are the person who directs it. There is no loss of control on your part in any sense. Instead, self-hypnosis is a means by which you can learn to have more control over your own thoughts, feelings, and actions than you currently possess. More will be said about self-hypnosis in the next chapter, which looks at self-hypnosis and relaxation in depth.

▶ What Is Hypnosis?

After reading about the four previously noted forms of hypnosis, you now have a good idea of what defines hypnosis. In summary, *hypnosis is a state of increased suggestibility, however it is attained.*

Hypnotists often refer to a conscious mind and to a subconscious mind in their work. The conscious mind includes that which you are aware of right now. It is your thinking mind, and because it has the capability of being analytical and critical, it can neutralize most suggestions. Unfortunately, the conscious mind often negates the value of positive suggestions as well. An example of this phenomenon occurs when you hear a compliment about your looks or your intelligence, and you think, "She doesn't really mean it," thereby preventing your self-esteem from increasing. Another clear example is when a friend encourages you to give up a bad habit, and you think, "Easy for him to say." In either instance, your conscious mind has negated the value of the positive suggestion.

In contrast, your subconscious mind does not have the ability to be critical. Instead, it is the part of your mind that works automatically and literally. The subconscious mind affects the way you function mentally and physically. One way that it affects you physically is through your autonomic nervous system, which controls your heart beat and breathing cycle when you are asleep. It affects you mentally by creating dreams for you, and by warehousing your deepest attitudes, values, beliefs, habits, and long-term memories. When you feel an emotion, it too, is created in your subconscious mind. When there is a conflict between the conscious mind and the subconscious mind, the subconscious mind wins. It is more primitive, but more powerful.

Try to stop feeling jealousy or envy, for example, if your mate dumps you for a more attractive and wealthier person. Try to stop feeling shame and guilt if you do something that goes against your values and beliefs. Try to stop nightmares by consciously dealing with an important issue in your life. Our subconscious mind works automatically, and it lets us know where we are *really* at with something.

If you don't really believe you can succeed at school, you'll be shocked at how the old failure scripts continue to play as you attempt to be successful. Likewise, when your deepest belief is that you will succeed, it's amazing how you will simply make yourself successful, despite the many challenges that school creates for you.

Because your conscious mind is limited by what you are thinking about now, it has a very limited capacity. The subconscious mind contains everything other than your present thoughts, and it has unlimited capacity. Your conscious mind is like the tip of an iceberg; most of it (i.e., your subconscious mind) lies beneath the surface.

Hypnosis results when your conscious mind takes a break (i.e., when it stops being critical and judgmental). Once it's on vacation (and hopefully not an extended one, like summer holidays), your subconscious mind automatically takes over. If what's inside your subconscious mind is positive, your goals become easier to accomplish. Why? Because the subconscious strives to create whatever lies within it. That doesn't mean that achieving important goals requires no effort. Instead, it means that you have two parts of your mind working toward the same goal, and thatthere is no internal conflict. For example, if you believe in recycling, and you get a job educating young people on this subject, you will feel a deep sense of meaning and purpose in what you are doing. A job becomes easier the more you deeply believe in its purpose. Contrast that feeling with how you would feel if you were completely against smoking, yet your job was to promote the interests of a tobacco company. That kind of predicament creates intense internal conflict.

▶ Dispelling the Myths About Hypnosis

The most common myths regarding hypnosis have to do with giving it magical qualities, including variations of either:
- the idea that the hypnotist is all powerful, or
- the belief that hypnosis itself is either all powerful or completely ineffective.

The Hypnotist Is All Powerful

On stage and in movies, hypnotists appear to have incredible control over their subjects. To the uninformed observer, hypnotists rule, and everyone else becomes a potential victim of their amazing mind control. Remember that stage hypnosis and clinical hypnosis occur only when the five Cs are in effect (i.e., cooperation, consent, concentration, communication, and conviction).

Hypnotists are either of the stage or the clinical variety, and therefore their ability and "power" over you are controlled by your desire to be hypnotized. Even then, you cannot be made to do things against your will. You do not lose consciousness when you are in hypnosis (unless you fall asleep, in which case you are no longer in hypnosis), and therefore, you hear everything being said to you. The moment you hear a suggestion that is disagreeable to you, you will reject it. If the suggestion is crazy enough, you will realize that the person is a charlatan, and you will end the hypnotic state yourself. You can always end a hypnotic state, or trance, on your own, so there is never a concern about what would happen if the hypnotist left you before ending the hypnotic session. You would simply end it yourself.

Research has shown that all hypnosis is really a form of self-hypnosis. If you want hypnosis, and are ready for it, only then will the conditions be right for it to occur. Otherwise, it just doesn't happen. Having said that, natural hypnosis does present interesting examples of times when people do influence us in all kinds of ways. Rarely are these people trained hypnotists. Our best defence is to keep our wits about ourselves when confronted by situations that make us more suggestible, like when we are tired or under the grip of an attractive salesperson.

Hypnosis Itself Is Either All Powerful or Completely Ineffective

If stage hypnosis were always effective, everyone who went up on stage would remain on stage. If clinical hypnosis were always effective, everyone treated by it would be cured of his or her problems, and no other treatment method would ever be necessary. Hypnosis is not the cure for everything. It has its limitations, and there are times when it doesn't work as hoped or as expected. The "magic" of clinical hypnosis is often the result of repetitive suggestions made at the appropriate times. Change also requires effort on the part of the person who wants the change. If you want to quit smoking, you will also have to find different ways of coping with stress and with many of your emotions. If you want to lose weight, suggestion alone will not substitute a healthy diet and an exercise program. Likewise, although self-hypnosis can help you become a more successful person and a better student, you will still need to work hard and study.

Another common misconception people have about hypnosis is that it can act as a lie detector test. The belief here is that, under hypnosis, you will automatically reveal your deepest secrets. Forget it—you can lie just as easily under hypnosis as you can at any other time. Closely related to this myth is another that many people hold: the idea that hypnosis can guarantee the accurate retrieval of long-forgotten details and memories.

Because of increased suggestibility, the mind will indeed attempt to recall things from the past if it is suggested. Due to many reasons that go beyond the scope of this book, memory cannot always be trusted, whether or not hypnosis has attempted to facilitate it. Psychologists know that memories are some-times *created* by our subconscious minds. These so-called "mem-ories" aren't real, although the person might believe them to be so. The technical term for such a false memory is a *pseudomemo-ry*. Because pseudomemories can be so damaging, hypnosis aimed at facilitating memory recall is not permitted in most crim-inal investigations today.

All of the above myths have the exaggerated power of either hypnosis itself or of the hypnotist as their theme. The remaining myth is the opposite of these myths—the idea that you are not suggestible, that you cannot be hypnotized, and that you will not, therefore, benefit from it. By now, you can appreciate that you have always been suggestible and that you always will be, particularly to that which can benefit you. If you found yourself in need of surgery, but were allergic to chemical anaesthetics, it would amaze you how much hypnosis could increase your sug-gestibility, which, in turn, would help your mind create the nec-essary numbness. Your mind is more powerful than anything you can imagine. Don't underestimate it, or yourself. You *can* change.

▶ Summary

Everyone has been hypnotized at some point. All of us have experienced times when we were more suggestible. The four forms of hypnosis include *natural hypnosis, stage hypnosis, clinical hypnosis,* and *self-hypnosis*. Hypnosis is an increased state of sug-gestibility, however it is attained. The conscious mind is what we are thinking about right now, and the rest of the mind is part of the subconscious. Hypnosis results when our conscious mind is bypassed, thus allowing the power of the subconscious to do its work. Tapping into this power is what the rest of this book is about.

Chapter Two

The Power of Self-Hypnosis and Relaxation

Imagine—just imagine. Where does your mind take you when you give it the freedom to go anywhere? The possibilities are endless in the world of imagination, in the world of daydreams and fantasies. The fact is, you have already imagined more wonderful ideas and experiences than you could ever achieve. So how do you take an idea from its inception to its realization? If you rely on life experience to change you, much of your control is lost to fate because many life experiences are not planned—they simply happen to you. How do you take constructive steps to change yourself while remaining in control of the process?

The Buddha is credited with saying, "We are what we think," meaning that the more we think about something, the more these thoughts come to define us, and the more likely we become to put these thoughts into action. Napoleon Hill, in his classic book, *Think and Grow Rich*, suggested that if you want to become rich, you need to think like a rich person thinks. As you begin to think in that particular way, you need to begin acting like a rich person acts. Getting to know rich people and spending as much time as possible with them are two of Hill's suggestions.

Psychologists James Prochaska, Norcross, and Diclemente (1994) argue that people go through predictable stages when they succeed in making personal changes. These psychologists support their arguments with an impressive amount of research conducted over many years. In their book, *Changing For Good*, they outline six necessary stages: precontemplation, contemplation, preparation, action, maintenance, and termination.

The precontemplation stage occurs before you think about making a specific change; while in the contemplation stage, you begin to think that making some kind of change is desirable. At this stage, however, you are not committed to taking any steps to change, and some people remain in the contemplation stage forever. For example, if you think about going to college someday but never do, you stay in the contemplation stage with respect to this desired change. In the preparation stage, you make thorough plans for making the change, and commit yourself to a start date. The plan will include the *what* and *how* of the change you intend to make, so a desire to attend college will require achieving necessary prerequisites in high school and having adequate financial resources, among many other necessary plans. The action stage is where you begin taking action toward your goal (e.g., applying for college), and the maintenance phase involves taking the necessary steps to continue succeeding at your goal (e.g., doing the homework, studying, and continuing to register for courses). The termination stage occurs when the goal has been fully realized (e.g., graduation).

What do the works of Napoleon Hill and James Prochaska et alii have to do with self-hypnosis? Referring to Hill's work, accomplishing an important goal requires that you become more like other people who have already accomplished the goal. If you want to become rich, think and act like a rich person. If you want to become a rock star, think and act like a rock star. Self-hypnosis can help you change your values, beliefs, or attitudes so that you begin to think more like the successful person you want to become.

Referring to Prochaska's work, we know that before you can achieve something, you first need to contemplate it. Self-hypnosis is an effective way of increasing your focus on a goal, and of intensifying the importance of that goal to you. Consequently, self-hypnosis can help you shorten the time you spend in contemplation by increasing your motivation to begin working on the goal, thereby launching you into the preparation and action phases. Self-hypnosis can also serve you well through the maintenance stage by helping you continue to keep your focus and to sustain your effort. Now let's take a closer look at self-hypnosis.

▶ Self-Hypnosis

How Does Self-Hypnosis Compare to Heterohypnosis?

As you discovered in Chapter 1, self-hypnosis is a relaxed state of increased suggestibility, which is both created and directed by you. It is often compared and contrasted to *heterohypnosis*, which, by the way, has nothing to do with being either straight or gay! Heterohypnosis is the term used when someone else hypnotizes you. Research undertaken in the 1970s revealed that both are the same altered state and that both are capable of producing the same desired results (see Fromm et al., 1981, Johnson, 1979, & Stanton, 1986). Some minor differences were noted, however, in how individuals subjectively experience hypnosis when they did it themselves as compared to when it was done to them. Compared to heterohypnosis, subjects in self-hypnosis have reported the following differences:

- enhanced imagery,
- fluctuating depth of trance,
- expansive attention and concentration,
- active direction,
- greater control.

During self-hypnosis, *imagery* becomes richer and more detailed. When you direct the activity of your mind, it can become more creative than if someone else directs it, similar to what happens when you are nearly asleep and beginning to dream.

The *depth of trance* is less stable in self-hypnosis as compared to heterohypnosis, especially when you are first learning it. The important thing to learn from this fact is not to worry if you have trouble attaining a deep state of relaxation at first. Remember— the subconscious mind takes over when you consciously stop trying, so if you try to make something happen intentionally, little will happen. Hypnosis occurs in the absence of effort, not as a consequence of it. Let things happen as they happen.

Attention and concentration are more focused in heterohypnosis compared to self-hypnosis, meaning that it is common for you to experience times in self-hypnosis where your attention drifts to something other than your goal. In this sense, your attention becomes more broad and less restrictive.

Compared to heterohypnosis, there is a sense of *directing*, rather than passively receiving suggestions while in self-hypnosis. Because you actively maneuver where your mind takes you, there is a greater awareness of having *control* while in a state of self-hypnosis.

What Does It Feel Like to Be in Self-Hypnosis?

Most people report feeling relaxed, carefree, and peaceful, while at the same time enjoying a general sense of well-being while in hypnosis (Edmonston, 1977). According to Holloway & Donald (1982), the sensations experienced during hypnosis include the kinesthetic (i.e., feelings of lightness, heaviness, warmth), the visual (i.e., lights, colors, shapes, images), and the tactile (i.e., the feeling of touches or breezes blowing across their bodies). In other words, being in hypnosis or self-hypnosis is a very pleasurable activity! Let's begin.

How Do I Enter Self-Hypnosis?

The instructions for entering self-hypnosis are found in Appendix 2. The two sections of Appendix 2 are called *Preliminary Practice* and *The Basic Induction Method*. Begin with the preliminary practice and do the exercises there until you feel competent using each of the three components of self-hypnosis. You also need to commit these components to memory before moving on to the basic induction method.

Next, begin practicing the basic induction method. The entire procedure need not take more than ten minutes, although most people will find fifteen to twenty minutes better for enhancing the depth of their relaxation. Once you are comfortable with the basic induction, you will be ready to begin using self-hypnosis for change as outlined in all of the subsequent chapters.

Are There Ways I Can Test My Suggestibility?

Yes, there are. There is really no need to do this because your mind will be motivated to make the changes that will help you academically.

Nonetheless, you might want to have some fun with the hypnotic tests outlined here. Before you start, be aware that hypnotic phenomena occur automatically while in a hypnotic state. Therefore, don't make the phenomena occur by forcing them, but on the other hand, don't stop the phenomena from occurring by holding back. Some people tell themselves things like, "It won't work," "It's not happening," or "What's wrong with me?" Remember: You become more suggestible to *all* suggestions in self-hypnosis, so self-defeating ones will surely take effect, and will prevent the desired response from occurring. Instead, the verbal suggestions you give yourself should be statements like, "It's beginning to work," "I can feel it happening," or "I am beginning to respond to this." The following are some common hypnotic tests:
- locked eyelids,
- arm rigidity,
- arm levitation.

Locked Eyelids

First, enter self-hypnosis using the basic induction method in Appendix 2. After step 5, press your eyelids together tightly, and give yourself the following suggestion, *"My eyelids are sealing togeth-er, glued together with Krazy Glue. They are sticking together tighter and tighter, tighter and tighter, and I can't open them. The harder I try, the tighter they stick together. My eyelids are now stuck firmly together."*

Now test your response by trying to open your eyelids. Keep telling yourself, *"They can't open no matter how hard I try,"* as you test them. After a minute or so of trying, stop testing yourself. If you couldn't open them, great! If you *could* open them, repeat the test until you respond correctly to it. If necessary, add in the visual image of having Krazy Glue applied to your eyelids. If you still don't respond after a few more attempts, review the thoughts you are telling yourself. You are probably counteracting the suggestion by telling yourself a self-defeating thought, such as, *"This can't possibly work."* In truth, it *will* work—if you stay focused on it. Before moving to the next test, remove the suggestions of locked eyelids by telling yourself, *"My eyelids are returning to normal, and I can again open my eyes."*

Arm Rigidity

First, enter self-hypnosis using the basic induction method in Appendix 2. After step 5, straighten your dominant arm (i.e., the one you write with) and make it tense and rigid. Holding this tension, give yourself the following suggestion,*"My arm is becoming a steel rod. It is becoming more and more and more straight. It is so rigid and hard, I cannot bend it. I cannot bend my arm. It has become steel, and the harder I try to bend it, the more straight and more rigid it becomes."*

Now test your response by trying to bend your arm. As you test it keep telling yourself, *"I can't bend my arm, no matter how hard I try."* After a minute or so of trying, stop testing yourself. If necessary, add in the visual image of seeing your arm turning into a steel rod. If you are still unsuccessful, continue in the same manner as was suggested in the locked eyelids test. Remember to remove the suggestion at the end of your testing by telling yourself, *"My arm is returning to normal, and I can again bend my arm."*

Arm Levitation

First, enter self-hypnosis using the basic induction method in Appendix 2. After step 5, let your dominant arm lie by your side, unobstructed, and focus your attention on your index finger, the finger next to your thumb. As you concentrate on your finger, think about how it already feels different from the other fingers in your dominant hand. Now give yourself the following suggestion, *"My finger is becoming so light it floats into the air. Helium balloons are being tied to this finger, and the finger is lifting upward. The finger is going up, up, up, up..."* Continue saying "up" to yourself until the finger lifts.

Now that the finger is lifting, we want to generalize that response to the rest of your hand. Now give yourself the following suggestion, *"Now helium balloons are being tied to all of the fingers and my thumb in this hand. I can feel my hand lifting, rising, lifting and rising. My hand is going up, up, up..."* Continue saying "up" to yourself until the hand lifts.

Now that the hand is lifting, we want to generalize that response to the rest of your arm, until your arm is floating above your head. Now give yourself the following suggestion, *"Now a tremendous hurricane is blowing underneath my hand, and underneath my elbow. My hand is lifting right up above my head, right up above my head. My arm is going up, up, up..."* Continue saying "up" to yourself until your arm lifts.

You will notice an interesting effect once your arm is suspended above your head. Your arm will feel as though it is weightless, and as though it could be suspended there indefinitely without any effort. A wonderful sensation, right? Again, remove the suggestion at the end of your testing by telling yourself, *"My arm is returning to normal, and it has become its normal weight once more."*

How Do I Use Self-Hypnosis To Make Changes?
Self-hypnosis relies on two approaches: verbal suggestions and visual imagery. Verbal suggestions are statements you make to yourself just before you enter self-hypnosis, once in self-hypno-

sis, or both. Visual imagery, on the other hand, is the use of our imagination to picture certain images, like we do when we day-dream. As mentioned in the Introduction, one method may work better for you than the other method, but you will only know by trying both methods. The way to use these methods is explained in Appendices 5 and 6.

A third approach is included in this book, and that approach is the use of a hypnotic script that you record. This method is most similar to heterohypnosis, except that it will be recorded in your own voice. One of the main advantages of making a tape or a digital recording is that it is once you have it prepared, it requires little to no effort to listen to it, whereas the other two methods require that you take a more directive role while in self-hypnosis.

When Should I Record and Begin Using the Hypnosis Tapes?

You can make these two recordings either now or after you finish reading this chapter. Begin by first reading Appendix 1, which shows you how to make these and all subsequent recordings. Once recorded, Major Script #1 (found in Appendix 3) will act as a relaxation tape and as a self-esteem booster, and it will help condition you to reach deeper stages of self-hypnosis. Major Script #2 contains suggestions and imagery for all of the important academic areas and personal growth areas. Once recorded, it becomes your generic student success tape.

Listen to your recording of Major Script #1 whenever you want to relax and whenever you want to condition yourself deeper for self-hypnosis. Another good time to listen to it is when your self-esteem feels diminished, or whenever you are feeling discouraged. Major Script #2 contains suggestions and imagery for all of the topics in this book, so you may want to listen to this recording frequently while you work through each chapter, and also whenever you feel you need a "booster shot" of positive thinking and motivation.

▶ Relaxation

Many busy people forget that spending time relaxing is an important part of leading a balanced life, and of managing their daily stresses. These same people often find that when they are ready to relax, they are unable to do so, either because they have never learned or never practiced it, or because they are literally too stressed to derive much benefit.

Relaxation is an important component of self-hypnosis, and in effect, *neutral hypnosis*, meaning hypnosis without suggestions or imagery, is the same thing as relaxation. As a student, you would do well to spend time relaxing as a daily practice. The first application of self-hypnosis in your studies, which will be described later, is simply using relaxation purposefully. There are significant documented benefits to using relaxation regularly.

What Are the Benefits of Relaxation?

The benefits of regular relaxation include positive physical, emotional, and cognitive changes. Here are a few examples:

Physical Benefits
- restorative function to the body
- improvement in health
- increased ability to cope with stress
- fewer medical symptoms
- improved sleep
- enhanced performance and efficiency
- decreased heart rate, blood pressure, respiration, and muscle tension

Emotional Benefits
- reduced worry and anxiety
- greater feelings of self-acceptance
- increased sense of purpose and satisfaction with life
- feelings of peacefulness

Cognitive Benefits
- improved memory and ability to concentrate
- reduction in self-critical, negative thoughts

In summary, relaxation not only makes you *feel* better, it actually *makes* you better in many areas of functioning. If you want to learn more about this topic, read Herbert Benson's book, *The Relaxation Response*. It is an interesting and well-researched book.

What Are the Different Methods of Relaxation?

There are many different methods of relaxation available today, and they all produce the same relaxation response as described by Herbert Benson. Some of these methods include meditation, yoga, self-hypnosis, progressive muscle relaxation, and auto-genic training. Autogenic training focuses on rhythmical breathing and feelings of warmth and heaviness throughout the body.

Which Method Should I Use?

The two methods described in this book are self-hypnosis and progressive muscle relaxation (PMR). If you find that you have trouble getting as relaxed as you want with self-hypnosis try PMR, which is the most popular method of relaxation taught. Recall the simultaneous muscle contraction you did earlier as part of the basic induction method for self-hypnosis. PMR is the same method; only it has you contract and relax each of your muscle groups sequentially, one by one. If you want to try this method, turn to Appendix 2 and record the complete script onto tape. Then as you listen to the tape, perform the muscle contractions and relaxations as suggested.

To summarize, whenever you want to practice relaxation, simply do one of the following activities:
- use the basic induction method found in Appendix 2,
- listen to your tape of Major Script #1 (i.e., Appendix 3),
- listen to your tape of progressive muscle relaxation (i.e., Appendix 7).

Using Relaxation to Become a More Effective Student

There are three times when using relaxation will help you as a student:

- as a daily practice,
- whenever you are under stress,
- to help you transition from your school to your home or your residence.

As a *daily* practice, relaxation will provide you the benefits listed earlier, including better concentration and memory and more positive thinking. Because relaxation is effective in reducing or eliminating anxiety, it is helpful to use at times when you are under *stress*.

You will notice one of the most immediate benefits of using relaxation when you start using it as a means of helping you make the *transition* from school to home. How many times have you felt too tired to study when you get home from school? This feeling of fatigue often lasts right up until bedtime! It also provides a great excuse for not to getting down to work. When you get home from school, studying is often the last thing you want to do because you are genuinely tired, and also because you have a negative attitude about what you need to accomplish, otherwise known as the "study blahs."

Fifteen to twenty minutes of relaxation can often feel like three hours of sleep when you are mentally fatigued, and it usually produces a more positive attitude as well. All you need to do is relax, using any of the relaxation methods already covered, at least twenty minutes before you intend to study, and presto—you are on your way!

▶ Summary

This chapter reviewed both self-hypnosis and relaxation. The two techniques of using self-hypnosis include verbal suggestions and visual imagery. Self-hypnosis with neither suggestion nor imagery is the same as relaxation. Three hypnotic tests were described for you to use if you want to have some fun with them.

The basic induction method for self-hypnosis is included in Appendix 2. Major Script #1, once recorded, is ideal for teaching you self-hypnosis and relaxation, whereas Major Script #2 covers the student success areas. Progressive muscle relaxation is another relaxation technique you can use, and its script in found in Appendix 7. Relaxation has many physical, emotional, and cognitive benefits. This chapter concluded by looking at how relaxation can help you succeed academically. If you haven't already recorded your major scripts or tried the progressive muscle relaxation, turn to the back of the book and do so now.

Part II

Applying the Four Powers of Success

Chapter Three

The Success Formula

Like many people who later become psychologists, I have spent my lifetime watching and observing people. I also read a lot. By the time I had completed ten years of university, I realized I had neither learned to study efficiently nor had I learned to manage my time very well. These are the two skills that most study guides emphasize. Despite having poor skills in these areas, I succeeded at school. I began questioning the idea that becoming a successful studen is primarily about developing exemplary time-management and study skills. Consequently, I came to some interesting conclusions about what underlies success.

What attributes distinguish those who are successful in school and in life, from those who are not? My answer, which is based on extensive observations and on my reading of psychology for the past thirty years, is what I call the *Success Formula*. The formula can be expressed in the form of an equation:

Success = $B^2 P^2$

B-squared stands for *Belief* and *Balance*, and P-squared stands for *Passion* and *Persistence*. In graphic form, the success formula is represented as follows:

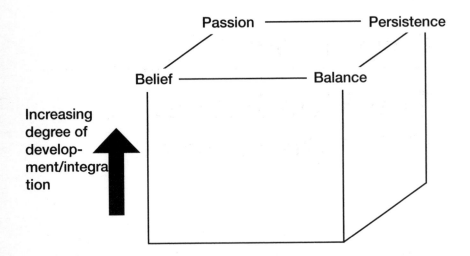

Along the left side of the figure is an upward arrow that signifies that each of these attributes can be developed in our lives to an optimal level. Theoretically at least, success becomes more likely as each attribute is further developed. Don't panic if you currently feel that you are lacking in any of these attributes. Even if you see yourself at the bottom of the cube in regard to all four attributes right now and feel like you are in the trenches of life, remember to look up at the stars and appreciate that you have no place to go but up—similar to how you feel after a night of serious partying! The next four chapters examine how each of the four attributes affects your life and how you can either begin or continue your growth in each area.

Chapter Four

The First Power: Belief (In Yourself)

I remember when I was working toward a master's degree in clinical psychology. I was nearing completion of the coursework and practicum, yet I still did not have a thesis topic. My thesis supervisor was also at his wits' end with me, so one day I received a letter in the mail stating that if I did not have a thesis proposal to him within six weeks, he would cease to continue in his role as my supervisor. I sat there shocked and scared. Deep in my mind I had harbored an unhealthy belief for several years: "I am not capable of doing a thesis. I can barely write a twenty-page essay, let alone a hundred-page thesis."

I started having night terrors while asleep. I would sit up in bed and scream. The worst instance was the night I got out of bed like a sleepwalker and checked under the bed for Martians while simultaneously screaming for my partner to leave the room and save herself! Luckily we were both saved when I finally came up with a topic. I then worked on the thesis for the next few months, and wrote the 200 pages that it required during the summer.

Soon after completing it my thesis, I sank into a deep clinical depression. I now know that a deep part of my mind was trying to prevent me from succeeding—the part of me that believed I was inadequate, inferior, and lacking. Now that my beliefs about myself have changed, I no longer scream in bed. Now I sleep without the demons of my own destruction.

Few people succeed in life without having a strong belief in themselves and in their capabilities. Examples abound of people who have accomplished great things despite facing incredible adversity. It is often said that successful people have faced as many failures as unsuccessful individuals. However, the successful people kept picking themselves up again while recommitting themselves to their goals.

Those who are not successful find ways to give up on themselves. I remember a childhood friend who was raised by an overly critical father. Whatever my friend did was never good enough. The constant putdowns hypnotized him to believe that he was lacking in many areas. I watched my friend over the years as he tried to succeed at his goals, but every time he got close to success, something would happen to jeopardize his efforts. When he returned to school several years later to upgrade his high school courses, he developed back trouble, and subsequently needed to drop out. However, this same individual was able to drive a school bus everyday, and his back never seemed to cause him much distress in this capacity. The last I heard, nothing had changed for my friend, other than that his complaints about his plight had become thirty years old!

Now ask yourself—how many times have you given up on a goal because you felt insecure, inferior, inadequate, or incapable? Don't get me wrong. We all have certain talents, just as we have relative weaknesses. It may be that you aren't capable of succeeding at your goal. If you want to become a nuclear physicist, you will need to have high intelligence and good aptitude in math. In other words, you also need to be realistic. Answering the questionnaire found in Appendix 9 will help you assess the cause of your inability to accomplish your goal. Although this question-naire refers to scholastic success, you could modify it to help you reflect on any goal that has not yet been attained.

A goal of this chapter will be to help you improve in the areas of self-esteem, self-concept, self-confidence, and self-efficacy. Self-esteem refers either to your global rating of yourself or to your judgment of some aspect of yourself. It refers to how you feel about yourself, so it usually has a valence: you either have positive self-esteem in an area you feel good about, or you have negative self-esteem in an area where you feel deficient. If you make a global rating, you either feel good about yourself in gen-eral, or you feel lacking.

Self-concept is related to self-esteem, but instead refers to the various identities that define who you are. For example, you might view yourself as intelligent, attractive, and sensitive. You might also define yourself as a skater, a basketball player, a sports enthusiast, a preppie, etcetera. All of these identifying qualities are aspects of your self-concept.

Self-esteem and self-concept are not always in sync either. You might view yourself as relatively unattractive (i.e., self-concept), however, you may feel that this quality is something you have no control over and view yourself very favorably despite this feeling (i.e., self-esteem).

The next concept is self-confidence, which is your current view of your capability of doing something. If you believe you have good skills in dating, you have self-confidence in this area. If you are shy, you probably lack dating confidence.

The final concept is self-efficacy. This concept includes both your anticipated view of your capability of doing something and your current view of your capability while developing the skill. Before you try something for the first time, you have a view as to whether you will be successful or not. The first time you danced, did you think you would be capable of dancing, or were you dreading the thought of possibly looking ridiculous because of your perception that you would fail miserably at the activity?

Furthermore, did you stop practicing dance moves because you didn't think that you could ever become capable? Lots of people don't dance because of low self-efficacy—and others shouldn't because they do look ridiculous out there.

Seriously though, as you come to believe in yourself more fully, you will experience:

• positive self-esteem in most areas,

• an accurate self-concept,

• appropriate self-confidence in skill areas you have developed,

• high self-efficacy in regard to most new activities.

Believing in yourself is crucial if you are going to succeed in school and in life. If you experience bonafide limitations, such as having lower intellectual capability or having a learning disability, school will be more of a struggle for you than for someone who is not similarly challenged. But my point is that with the right belief system, you will optimize your capabilities, and without the right belief system, it won't matter how smart or capable you are—you won't use the many talents given to you anyway.

▶ Conventional Methods of Fostering Belief

Whether you are in need of developing an accurate self-concept or of improving your self-esteem, self-confidence, self-efficacy, or some combination thereof, realize that at the root of your problem is the way that you view yourself. Most often, whether you see the proverbial cup as half empty or half full is simply a matter of self-perception. Changing the way you look at things can be achieved in several ways, but the most established techniques are derivatives of cognitive therapy as developed by Albert Ellis, Aaron Beck, and Donald Meichenbaum. The premise of cognitive therapy is that the way we look at things determines how we feel about them. If we entertain plenty of negative thoughts, we will experience plenty of negative feelings. The converse is also true—positive thoughts lead to positive emotions.

One of the biggest obstacles to developing a positive belief system is perfectionism. Remember the cliché, *No one is perfect.* Perfectionists acknowledge the truth in this statement, however, they continue to indoctrinate themselves into believing that doesn't really apply to them. Some perfectionists are disappointed when they only get ninety percent on a test! The best solution to perfectionism is to work on accepting the idea that you are striving for competence, not perfection. Competent individuals still make mistakes, and they accept themselves whenever they do.

Doing cognitive therapy on yourself is straightforward, and you can use the triple-column shown below to begin your work (a sample is provided).

MALADAPTIVE THOUGHT OR BELIEF	QUESTIONING IT	HEALTHY THOUGHT OR BELIEF
"I am good for nothing. I will never do well in math."	"Why do I believe this? Just because I failed a math exam doesn't mean I am no good. In my case, it means I didn't study enough and I didn't answer enough practice questions. I need to work harder and smarter."	"I am a worthwhile person, but I need to work harder at math if I am going to do better at it."

This is how you use the triple-column:

1. *Brainstorm your bad thoughts.* In the first column write out the thought(s) or belief(s) causing you to feel badly about yourself. You might already be aware of some of these thoughts, in which case you can record them now. Another approach is to wait until something triggers you to feel badly before making an entry.

2. *Challenge yourself.* In the second column, challenge the logic behind the thought or belief. Use the questions below to help you do this:

a) What proof do I have that this is true?

b) Do I have any evidence that indicates it is not true?

c) Are there any competing "truths?" Is another belief just as valid?

d) Does everyone think this way? Why not?

e) Does agreeing with the majority on this make it necessarily correct?

f) Where did I learn this message? Is it possible that the messenger was wrong?

g) What purpose is served in continuing to believe this?

h) What price do I pay for continuing to believe this?

i) What will be the advantages of believing something different?

j) Are my feelings about this providing an accurate gauge of what I should believe?

k) If I was helping someone else deal with this, what would I want him to believe?

l) If I knew I would be dead tomorrow, would I be happy believing this?

Once you have challenged your thinking, write out the challenge in the second column.

3. *Turn things around.* In the third column, write out a healthy version of the thought(s) or belief(s) that you would like to substitute for the one written in the first column.

4. *Focus on the third column.* Spend time focusing on the

thought(s) or belief(s) written in the third column. The more you absorb yourself in repeating the thought(s) or belief(s) in column three, the more you will internalize the message.

5. *Repeat when necessary.* Whenever you catch yourself repeating similar negative thoughts to yourself, either write them down again and repeat steps 2 through 5 of the previous list, or do the work in your head by talking to yourself, either silently or out loud. Remember to do both the challenge and then to substitute the healthy thought or belief.

Here are a few other ideas for improving your self-esteem, as suggested by Weiten and Lloyd (2003):

1. *Be aware that you are in control.* Self-esteem is something that you need to control. Although others will give you feedback about aspects of yourself, you are ultimately the one who must decide how to view yourself. It is you who maintains your self-image.

2. *Develop greater self-awareness.* You will improve your self-esteem by learning more about yourself. As this is an important part of *passion*, this topic will be covered in depth in Chapter 4.

3. *Set your own goals.* You cannot follow someone else's path in life: you must find your own way. As you begin to walk in your own shoes, you will appreciate yourself more fully.

4. *Recognize when your goals are unrealistic.* If your goals are set too high, you will only experience frustration and disappointment. Be sure to take an accurate stock of your capabilities and limitations before embarking on an arduous path. If necessary, seek opinions from those people who know you well if you are having trouble making an accurate assessment, or seek the advice of a psychologist.

5. *Change negative self-talk.* Review the triple column preceding this section for help with this problem.

6. *Emphasize the strengths you have.* One method of improving your self-esteem is to spend more time focusing on your strengths than on your weaknesses. Remember that what you feed your mind will impact how you feel about yourself, and it

will impact how you feel about everything else as well.

7. *Treat others in a positive manner.* Weiten and Lloyd suggest that one of the best ways to feel good about yourself is to be validated by others who respect and like you. The more you show genuine like, respect, and affection for others, the more this treatment will be reciprocated.

As self-esteem problems are common, below are some additional resources that you may find useful if you want to use additional conventional methods are listed below (as suggested by "The University of Texas at Austin," 1999):

• Burns, D. D. (1999). *Ten Days to Self-Esteem.* New York: Quill.

• James, M., & Jongeward, D. (1996). *Born to Win: Transactional Analysis with Gestalt Experiments.* Boulder, CO: Perseus Press.

• Johnson, K., & Ferguson, T. (1991). *Trusting Ourselves: The Complete Guide to Emotional Well-Being for Women.* New York: Atlantic Monthly Press.

• McKay, M., & Fanning, P. (2000). *Self-Esteem: A Proven Program of Cognitive Techniques for Assessing, Improving and Maintaining Your Self-Esteem.* Oakland, CA: New Harbinger.

• Seligman, M. (1998). *Learned Optimism: How to Change Your Mind and Your Life.* New York: Pocket Books.

▶ Self-Hypnosis Applications
The Clenched Fist Technique

The clenched fist technique was developed by Stein (as cited in Stanton, 1988), and was intended to help people overcome a plethora of negative feelings. You too can use it for the same reasons, and I present it here as a way of improving self-esteem. Here are the steps to conditioning yourself to use the technique:

1. *Hypnotize yourself.* Use the basic induction (see Appendix 2).

2. *Relax and recall.* Once you are deeply relaxed, remember a situation in the past where you experienced positive self-esteem.

3. *React.* As you recall how you felt at that past time, clench the fist of your dominant hand and give yourself the following suggestion: "Whenever I clench this fist in the future, I will re-expe-

rience a surge in positive self-esteem."

4. *Double the impact.* Think of another time in the past when you experienced positive self-esteem.

5. *Repeat.* Repeat the action and phrase from step 3.

6. *Confront.* Next, remember a situation in the past where you experienced diminished self-esteem.

7. *React.* As you recall how you felt at that time, clench your non-dominant hand into a fist and imagine the negative feelings flowing into it.

8. *Combine.* Now link the two parts of the procedure by first clenching your dominant fist and focusing on positive self-esteem.

9. *Let go.* Now clench your non-dominant fist and allow it to open, letting the negative feelings associated with diminished self-esteem to flow away and evaporate into nothingness.

10. *Finish.* Whenever you are ready, exit the self-hypnotic state.

Now that you have begun to condition yourself to use the technique, here is how you use it:

• Whenever you feel diminished self-esteem in your daily life, stop what you are doing and clench both fists.

• If you can close your eyes for a few moments, do so. If not, proceed to the next step.

• Feel the surge of positive self-esteem through your dominant fist while opening your non-dominant fist, thus allowing the negative feelings to dissipate.

• Now open your eyes if they were closed and carry on with your activities.

You will need to strengthen the response periodically by repeating the ten conditioning steps while in self-hypnosis. I suggest doing it daily at first until the response is firmly established.

Suggestions/Affirmations
(Note: instructions for using suggestions/affirmations are found in Appendix 6.)

1. I strive to be competent and I accept that I occasionally make mistakes.

2. I am developing an accurate picture of my strengths and weaknesses.

3. I focus on mostly positive thoughts about myself.

4. I feel my self-confidence increasing as I develop new skills and improve old ones.

5. I approach new tasks with feeling capable.

[Write some of your own below]:

6.

7.

8.

Imagery

(Note: instructions for using imagery are found in Appendix 5.)

Begin by writing down circumstances, situations, or events that have already proven themselves to be capable of lowering your self-esteem, self-confidence, or self-efficacy. Then imagine yourself doing these things competently in detail.

For example, if you lack confidence in asking someone out on a date, repeatedly visualize yourself doing this with finesse. Also in your imagery, imagine the words you might use in making the approach. If you have been earning low grades and you have determined that the main reason is insufficient time spent studying, picture yourself studying for longer periods of time while enjoying the fact that you are learning new material.

If you are afraid to try something new or if you anticipate that you will not be successful, visualize yourself learning the new activity in a step-by-step fashion. See each step to learning the activity in as much detail as possible while maintaining a positive enthusiastic attitude.

Script

[CAUTION: *If you have a medical condition or physical problem that might prevent you from doing any of the exercises contained in this script, please use a pencil and cross out the part of the script that contains these exercises. If you are uncertain about whether to exclude something, ask your physician before making this self-hypnosis tape. Also remember that the scripts are to be recorded verbatim, as described in Appendix 1. Instructions for using the pause conventions, which are enclosed in square brackets in the script and not recorded, are found in Appendix 1.]*

"Get comfortable, preferably lying down with your arms and legs uncrossed. Now contract all of your muscles simultaneously, and hold the tension [pause for seven breaths]. Now relax your muscles, and notice the contrast between muscle tension and relaxation [pause for four breaths]. Now contract all of your muscles simultaneously again, and hold the tension [pause for seven breaths]. Now relax your muscles, and notice the contrast once more [pause for 4 breaths].

"With your eyes open, roll your eyes upward slightly (i.e., toward your forehead) so that you feel a mild eye strain, and then stare at a spot while keeping your eyes in that position. Do not let your gaze drift from that spot. Take five deep abdominal breaths [pause for two breaths]. Inhale the fifth breath extra deeply, and while holding it, count backwards mentally, '5-4-3-2-1.' When you get down to '1,' exhale and close your eyes at the same time [pause for two breaths].

"Every day you find yourself becoming mentally healthier and stronger [pause for one breath]. You feel increasingly positive about who you are and the person you are becoming [pause for one breath]. You are letting go of perfectionistic tendencies and replacing these with a desire to be competent [pause for one breath]. This means you forgive yourself when you make mistakes, but you also learn from them so as to reduce the probability of making the same mistakes again [pause for two breaths].

"As you develop greater competence, you also become increasingly self-confident [pause for one breath]. Your self-confidence steadily improves [pause for one breath]. You look forward to learning new skills and having new experiences [pause for one breath]. When you begin learning something new, you maintain a good feeling about your capability [pause for one breath]. Learning something new takes time and no one, especially yourself, expects you to be competent from the very beginning [pause for one breath]. You are a reasonable person, and you are reasonable with yourself [pause for two breaths].

"In every way each day, you become more of who you are, and less of who others are or who others want you to be [pause for one breath]. This is your life, and you need to find your own path—a road that will take you where you want to go [pause for two breaths].

"When you are ready to leave self-hypnosis, first silently tell yourself that you will count to five and that at the count of five you will come out of self-hypnosis feeling refreshed, relaxed, and confident [pause for one breath]. Then awaken yourself by counting to five mentally, and say 'AWAKE!' to yourself [pause for three breaths]. Then open your eyes."

▶ Summary

This chapter has shown you how to develop *belief*, the first power of success. Learning to believe strongly in yourself entails developing positive self-esteem and an accurate self-concept. It also means becoming self-confident and developing a respect for your ability to learn new things.

Chapter Five

The Second Power: Passion

I used to watch the old Bob Newhart series in which he played a psychologist. Although his clients were often nutty, he wasn't. Instead, Bob was the kind of person I admired: intelligent, witty, responsible, and well-adjusted. I wanted to be like him. As I entered late adolescence, my desire to become a psychologist grew stronger.

I remember that at the age of nineteen I convinced myself that I needed to become a sex therapist. One could argue that raging hormones had a lot to do with my interest back then. I talked to every professor who might know how I could achieve this goal, and I enrolled in every sex course I could find. My passion intensified as I continued on through my graduate studies, and despite many obstacles along the way, I continued my training. I became a hypnotherapist before I became a licensed psychologist, and then I worked in a community college for many years where questions about sexuality seemed remarkably rare. Now I am a professor, and my primary research specialty is sexuality. I also do some work in private practice. Strange how my passion to become a sex therapist has finally realized itself—nearly thirty years later.

Have you ever wanted something so badly that you would have done almost anything to get it or to achieve it? If not, then you have yet to experience passion. *Passion* is a deep-rooted belief and commitment toward a particular goal or ideology. Passion is generally accompanied by emotion, both when thinking and talking about whatever makes you passionate, but perhaps, especially when it is being thwarted in some way. In some religious circles, they refer to what makes you passionate as your "calling." When you have passion, you feel energized as you think about, and begin pursuing your target. Underlying passion is a belief that the goal or ideology has deep meaning or significance to you.

Accomplishing a goal without passion is a bit like having to clean your bedroom because your mom tells you to. You might know it is the right thing to do, but doing it feels like soulless work. All you can think about is the relief of getting finished.

Terry Fox was a man who felt great passion about raising money for cancer research. He became so focused on his goal that he kept running while his body was succumbing to yet another bout with cancer. He never finished the run—he collapsed before his unwilling body would take him where his mind so wanted to go. Terry passed away on June 28, 1981—one month before his twenty-third birthday.

Passion is an attribute of most heroes, and it is an important attribute underlying greatness. We admire passionate people because they remind us that there are things in life that are worth pursuing with vigor and dedication.

How do you become passionate? Passion is intimately connected with knowing yourself and having a strong sense of your own identity. Many young people choose careers without having deep insight into what makes them tick. It should come as no surprise then that youths between the ages of fifteen and twenty-four in Canada are the least likely to indicate that they are very satisfied with their work ("Canadian Institute for Health Information," 1999) compared to those over twenty-four years of age. To develop passion, the following seems to be necessary:

- you must have a clear sense of your identity, including your likes and dislikes,
- you need to set goals based on your identity, and then prioritize these goals,
- the highest priority goals must be deeply meaningful to you in some way.

If you are not feeling passionate about where your education is taking you, even if you are still in grade school, it is difficult to sustain the effort required to attend classes and earn good grades while you do so. I suspect that this is one of the biggest reasons why some students drop out of high school and fail to attain good positions in life. The dropout who goes on to greatness is by far the exception rather than the rule.

This chapter will look at the ways you can begin getting a clearer sense of your identity. It will also look at goal setting and how to make your top goals more meaningful. As this develops, you will find more of the passion you need to become truly successful in school, and in life.

▶ Conventional Methods of Fostering Passion
Enhance Self-Awareness

1. *Self-Examination.* Come to know yourself better. How? Come to know yourself by exploring personal experiences, listing your likes and dislikes, listing your admirable traits and less admirable traits, and listing your values. Your career choice or career planning may also shed some insights. Which jobs do you most admire? Why? If you had no limitations, what career would you choose? An excellent free resource from the University of Waterloo regarding career planning can be found at http://www.cdm.uwaterloo.ca

2. *Psychological Testing.* A personality test, like the Myers-Briggs Type Indicator (MBTI) or the Strong Interest Inventory (SII) may prove helpful. You should be able to take these tests through the counseling center at your school. (Note: these tests

are not very useful until you are at least sixteen years of age.) At the date of this book's publication, there were two free versions of the MBTI available on the Internet: http://typefocus.com (under Free Personality Assessment) and www.humanmetrics.com/cgi-win/Jtypes1.htm If you are unable to access these helpful sites, try conducting an online search of your own.

Purpose of Life

What gives your life meaning? What is most important to you? How do you want to make a difference? Think of the most meaningful experience you have had in your life. What made it so meaningful? List your answers.

Becoming Independent in Your Thinking

Focus on personal empowerment. This is the time to be a nonconformist—you will never find your passion so long as you depend on or care about what others think of your choices.

Establish Goals for Yourself

If you don't know what you want, or what you're trying to accomplish, it's difficult to feel passion or motivation toward anything that you do. You must perceive that the benefits that you will derive from your goal will outweigh the costs of attaining it. Any worthwhile goal is going to take some work to accomplish.

Setting Goals

Think about a goal you have already accomplished—one that you chose. How did you attain that goal? Chances are you achieved your goal by following this standard pattern for success:

1. An idea for a possible goal enters your mind (e.g., thinking about joining the basketball team).

2. You learn about and consider the pluses and minuses of pursuing that goal (e.g., "How much time will it take for the practices and games? Can I afford it? Do I have enough skill?").

3. You decide on the goal (e.g., "Yes, I want to get on the team").

4. You take steps to begin pursuing the goal (e.g., try out for the team).

5. You remain persistent (e.g., "I didn't get on this year. After another year of practice, I'll try again").

6. You continue pursuing the goal (e.g., "Finally, I'm on the team").

7. You stay committed (e.g., "I will not quit halfway through the ball-playing season").

Principles of Goal Setting
Your goals must:

1. *Be your own personal goals.* Until you establish and internalize your own goals, they will lack meaning and you will lack sufficient drive to attain them.

2. *Be realistic and attainable.* There is no point in setting goals that are impractical. Unrealistic goals will only frustrate and disappoint you.

3. *Be clearly defined.* If you want to exercise more, write out exactly what it is you want to do. For example, "I will ride the exercise bike three times a week for twenty minutes on Mondays, Wednesdays, and Fridays."

4. *Have a deadline for achievement.* Write out your goals and establish deadlines for their achievement. This will help you minimize procrastination.

Setting Priorities
No single goal is unfulfillable. Attempting to accomplish everything at once, however, is not realistic. Consequently, you need to establish your priorities. Give all of your goals a rank order (i.e., your most important goal is number one, your second most important goal is number two).

Develop a Strong Desire to Accomplish Your Goals

The one major reason a lot of people express the feeling that their goals are unfulfillable is because they don't desire them strongly enough. The more time you spend focusing on a goal, the stronger it becomes.

Using Role Models

Look for a role model who has already achieved one or more of your important life goals. The role model could be fictitious, the way Bob Newhart's portrayal of a psychologist was my role model, or he or she could be an actual person, either living or dead. Then, engage with your role model in some way. For example, if your role model is a television character, watch the character in his or her television series. If the role model is a historical figure, read as much as you can about this person. If you have a goal to become more fit or healthier, paste up photographs of fit and healthy individuals in noticeable places. If you already know someone in your life who can act as a role model, even better. Spend time with this person and let him or her know that you want to achieve a similar or identical goal.

▶ Self-Hypnosis Applications
Suggestions/Affirmations

(Note: instructions for using suggestions/affirmations are found in Appendix 6.)

1. I am dedicated to learning more about my likes and dislikes.

2. I am becoming more of who I am and less of what others want me to be.

3. More of my time and energy is being devoted to finding my passions in life.

4. My career choice will (or does) reflect some of my deepest passion.

5. I pay attention to role models and mentors to learn what I can from them.

[Write some of your own]:

6.

7.

8.

Imagery
(Note: instructions for using imagery are found in Appendix 5.)

Gaining a Clearer Sense of Your Identity
If you were to die tomorrow, what would you want to be remembered for? After visualizing what you would want, list these qualities, traits, accomplishments, etcetera. Related to this visualization activity is imagining what a typical day would look like at work if you had complete control over it. Later write down some of the aspects that you imagined would make that a good day. Another visual image is created by imagining how you would spend your day if you didn't have to work—what would you be doing instead? What is it that really excites you in life?

Setting Your Goals
If you are having trouble setting your goals and prioritizing them using conventional methods, try spending time visualizing yourself in numerous situations to get some sense of whether you might want to establish any of these experiences as goals. For example, let's pretend that you are thinking about bodybuilding, but you aren't sure if you would like that activity. Visualize yourself going to a gym, imagine the equipment inside, and picture yourself lifting weights. Don't forget to also imagine your body as it becomes more muscular. As you begin to imagine more and more possibilities, you will also develop a sense of what priority to give each goal.

Increasing Dedication and Desire For Your Goals
The best technique to increase dedication and desire for your goals is to visualize their outcome. Stay focused on seeing how different aspects of your life change as you achieve goals. If your goal is to become a more caring person for example, picture yourself doing caring activities, and allow a nurturing feeling and a

feeling of compassion to emerge as you continue to visualize. The more you imagine the outcome will look like when the goal is achieved, the more you set in motion the desire to make it happen. Do this often as a way of strengthening your passion and your motivation.

Script

[CAUTION: *If you have a medical condition or physical problem that might prevent you from doing any of the exercises contained in this script, please use a pencil and cross out the part of the script that contains these exercises. If you are uncertain about whether to exclude something, ask your physician* before *making this self-hypnosis tape.*]

"Get comfortable, preferably lying down with your arms and legs uncrossed. Now contract all of your muscles simultaneously, and hold the tension [pause for seven breaths]. Now relax your muscles, and notice the contrast between muscle tension and relaxation [pause for four breaths]. Now contract all of your muscles simultaneously again, and hold the tension [pause for seven breaths]. Now relax your muscles, and notice the contrast once more [pause for four breaths].

"With your eyes open, roll your eyes upward slightly (i.e., toward your forehead) so that you feel a mild eye strain, and then stare at a spot while keeping your eyes in that position. Do not let your gaze drift from that spot. Take five deep abdominal breaths [pause for two breaths]. Inhale the fifth breath extra deep, and while holding it, count backwards mentally, '5-4-3-2-1.' When you get down to '1,' exhale and close your eyes at the same time [pause for two breaths].

"You are motivated to know yourself more fully [pause for one breath]. You embrace the uniqueness that makes you who you are, and coming to know your likes and dislikes feels gratifying [pause for one breath]. Knowing that you don't need to like everything or everyone is, in fact, liberating [pause for one breath]. Becoming your own person allows you to love the things and the people that really matter [pause for one breath]. You know that you will make a difference in this life—your impact will be felt [pause for one breath]. Underlying the difference that you will make is great passion toward important life goals [pause for one breath]. Increasingly, you find yourself become a passionate individual, a person who strives toward your own commitments and beliefs [pause for two breaths].

"Your goals are becoming ever more crystallized and ever more real [pause for one breath]. The more you focus on them, the more important they become to you [pause for one breath]. You deserve to succeed in school and in life [pause for one breath]. This is, after all, your life, and no one but you can achieve what is important to you [pause for one breath]. You are continually coming to better terms with your priorities, and acting on them accordingly [pause for two breaths].

"Your most important goals take on deep and personal meaning [pause for one breath]. They may not have meaning to other people, and that is fine [pause for one breath]. It is enough that your goals serve your own purposes in life [pause for one breath]. The more you focus on any particular goal, the more it becomes realized [pause for one breath]. Your passion toward your important goals sustains you during times of dedicated effort [pause for one breath]. Nothing important ever occurred to anyone without dedication and perspiration [pause for one breath]. You are up for the fight—you are a passionate individual [pause for two breaths].

"When you are ready to leave self-hypnosis, first silently tell yourself that you will count to five and that at the count of five, you will come out of self-hypnosis feeling refreshed, relaxed, and confident. Then awaken yourself by counting to five mentally, and say 'AWAKE!' to yourself [pause for three breaths]. Then open your eyes."

▶ Summary

In this chapter you learned how to develop the second power of success: *passion*. To develop passion, you need to have a clear understanding of your likes and dislikes. In other words, you need to know yourself. Besides this, you also need to establish realistic goals and decide on their priority to you. The final part of developing passion is to increase the desire you have to attain your goals.

Chapter Six

The Third Power: Persistence

At the college where I once worked, I hypnotized hundreds of students, both individually and in groups. I witnessed their enjoyment of being hypnotized and the benefits they repeatedly derived from it. The thought of writing this book occurred to me many times over the past seventeen years, and I even told some people about my idea. None of them ever thought I would do it: In truth, neither did I.

I needed to look at the many half read books on my bookshelves and uncompleted projects on my desk and in my mind before I realized the pattern I had established. I knew that successful individuals don't start endless projects without finishing at least some of those endeavors.

I remember signing a contract with one of my Ph.D. supervisors that said that I would co-author an article with her upon the completion of my dissertation. That was in 1996. I felt some guilt that I never fulfilled that contract. In 2001, I finally lived up to my obligation and I wrote the article, but it didn't get published. Two years later, I worked on a different co-authored article. I sensed, at this point, that my Ph.D. supervisor didn't believe that I would complete it, but eventually the article did get published— and my supervisor was already retired by that point!

...However, now you are reading *Grade Power* many years after the idea was conceived. I have learned that if you want to write a book—write it—and don't stop until it's done. The same is true of other important life goals. The point is, some projects need to get accomplished, and "better late than never."

How many times have you felt excited about pursuing a goal, only to find that your motivation dwindled before the goal could be completed? How many half-done projects do you have in your life right now?

Persistence is about pursuing your goal, even in the face of adversity. The result of persistence is the completion of a goal or task. I generally prefer the term *persistence* rather than the term *motivation* because most of us see motivation as having an emotional element. In other words, when we are motivated to do something, we often say that we *feel* motivated. Relying on feelings to get something done is fraught with difficulty. How often do you actually *feel* like doing your homework? How often do you feel like doing anything that is difficult or time consuming? "Rarely" would be the answer, I suspect.

It is easy to procrastinate regarding tasks that we find undesirable in some way. If you procrastinate, you may eventually get the job done, but you will end up motivating yourself through fear. However, fear will deplete your energy reserves and this can exhaust you if it continues for too long. Furthermore, if you end up procrastinatingregarding studying, you will likely end up "cramming" the night before an exam, which often has negative consequences with respect to your grade.

In this chapter, I will show you ways to stop procrastinating and ways to develop the kind of impenetrable determination that underlies persistence. Be sure to use the conventional methods in this chapter, as the discipline required for persistence is often best developed through a structured approach. Also be aware that your persistence will be greater when you already have a strong belief in your ability to succeed (i.e., Chapter 4) and when you have developed passion for your goals (i.e., Chapter 5).

▶ Conventional Methods of Fostering Persistence
Overcoming Procrastination

Procrastination occurs when we don't want to do something, often because we see the task before us as difficult, time-consuming, unpleasant, or some combination thereof. Here are some suggestions to help you break the cycle of procrastination:

Chipping the Ice

The best way to approach a difficult and time-consuming task is to break it down into smaller, more manageable steps, a practice I call *chipping the ice*. For example, no one climbs Mount Everest in a day, you need to plan each aspect of the excursion carefully and then ascend over a requisite duration of time.

Now to use a more academically-relevant example, let's say you have a thirty-page essay due in a month. This task could seem especially daunting if you have poor writing skills. Let's begin breaking this assignment down into doable steps:

1. Conduct a thorough search, using electronic databases, for articles and books on the essay topic. Also check the library catalogue for relevant books (complete in the next three days).

2. Collect relevant books and photocopy required articles (complete in the next two days).

3. Read all articles and relevant sections from the books and take notes (complete in the next seven days).

4. Write out an outline for the essay (complete in two days). Imagine in this example that the outline has five sections.

5. Take two days to write out each section of the essay respectively—each section will be about six pages (complete in ten days).

6. Ask a friend who has good writing skills to edit your essay (complete in three days).

7. Don't look at the essay for two days. After that time you might see other changes you want to make (two days).

8. Read the entire paper and make any further edits you think will improve the essay (complete in one day).

9. Submit the completed essay.

Using Rewards

Chipping the ice works well when a task is seen as difficult and/or time-consuming. If you also see the task as unpleasant, yet necessary, then you need to rely on the use of a reward system. A reward is simply treating yourself to something you find pleasurable for accomplishing a certain task. Reward yourself after completing step 1, for instance, and again after completing step 2. A reward should be something that is readily available to you, and probably something that you do on a periodic basis anyway.

You might be thinking, "Well, if I do it anyway, how is that rewarding?" The important point is not to give yourself the reward until *after* you complete the task. If the task does not get completed as planned, the reward is withheld until it is completed. Include the duration that you will enjoy the reward as well. Here are some good examples of rewards:

- taking a walk (one hour),
- telephoning or chatting online with a friend (fifteen minutes),
- relaxing on the couch (twenty minutes),
- watching a favourite television program (thirty minutes),
- listening to music (twenty minutes),
- partaking in an engaging hobby (forty-five minutes),
- enjoying a tanning session (fifteen minutes),
- cycling around a city park (forty minutes),
- cooking a gourmet meal (two hours),
- enjoying a hot cup of tea or coffee (ten minutes).

There are two systems by which to reward yourself: *time-based rewards* and *task-based rewards*. Using a time-based reward system, you give yourself a break and a reward after a specified amount of time working on the task at hand. Using a task-based reward system, you don't take a break or give yourself a reward until a segment of a task, or the entire task, is first completed.

Getting Organized for the Semester

You need to get organized if you are going to become persistent in working on your goals. The following sheets will be helpful:

Semester Timetable Sheet

Begin your organization of the term or semester by using the *Semester Timetable* sheet found on the next page. It is set up for sixteen weeks of classes and exams—if your term is longer than four months, use a second sheet and attach it. Here is how you use the sheet:

1. Write out the dates for the weeks of the term in the first column (e.g., the first entry might be "Sep. 13–17," then "Sep. 20–24" below this, and so forth).

2. Next, write in the Monday through Friday columns when your exams and quizzes are scheduled to occur, and also write in when your assignments and papers are due. Also include what percentage of your final grade each entry is worth. For example, let's say you have a midterm for biology on October 20 worth 25 percent of your final grade. Write in the appropriate column and row, "BIOLOGY 201 midterm, 25%."

3. Keep the Semester Timetable Sheet at the front of your binder so that you can review it periodically and use it for planning purposes.

Time Commitments Sheet

This sheet will help you determine how many hours you will likely need to study for a post-secondary education if you want to earn top grades. It is based on the commonly-held belief that a student of average ability should spend two hours outside of class in study and in course preparation for every hour of class time. As not everyone is of average ability, the *Scholastic Ability Multiplier* at the top of the sheet will help you determine what is right for you.

For example, if you have superior ability or intellect, you can reduce the number of study and preparation hours to one hour for every hour of class time. Alternatively, if you have below-average scholastic ability or if you have a learning disability, you will need to increase the number of academic hours. I know that you might not know where you are at in terms of your ability, especially if you have not been succeeding scholastically. Begin by answering the questionnaire in Appendix 9. If you are still uncertain, do not hesitate to book an appointment with your school or guidance counselor for help determining your ability level.

At the bottom of the *Time Commitments Sheet* is the recommended maximum number of hours you should be spend working, if you need to work in addition to attending school. Following these guidelines will help prevent you from feeling overloading. If you are working too many hours at school and at a job, you run the risk of burnout, which effectively means you are exhausted and rendered less effective in your efforts to succeed (see the next chapter about keeping balance in your life).

Getting Organized Weekly

Two methods are suggested in this section that will help you get down to work and persist in that that work. Although the methods are similar, you might prefer one more than the other.

Method #1: Typical

Most study guides suggest that you complete a *Weekly Timetable* sheet as well. An example is provided in this chapter. Here is how you use it:

1. *Acknowledge existing structure.* Begin by blocking in all of the "fixed" times in your schedule—your classes, your work schedule (if it is consistent every week), your lab times, meals, fitness schedule, etcetera—in ink.

2. *Build on it.* Next, using a pencil, block in your planned study times, remembering to base this on your calculations from the Time Commitments Sheet.

3. *Relax and reward.* Where you have planned to do academic work for more than thirty minutes, remember to take breaks periodically. Establish rewards for getting a certain amount of work done if you find the task paticularly difficult, time-consuming, and/or unpleasant.

Now that you have created your Weekly Timetable sheet, you are ready to make entries into the *Academic Do List*. Here is how you use the Academic Do List:

1. *Engineer.* If in the Weekly Timetable sheet you wrote that you are going to do academic work for three hours on Monday, and it *is* Monday, begin the day by writing down precisely what you intend to do during those three hours. Be as specific as possible. For example, it could look like the following: (1) Work on math problems (time allotted: 1 hour); (2) Research essay topic in the library (time allotted: 1.5 hours); and (3) Study chapter 6 in biology textbook (time allotted: 30 minutes).

2. *Execute.* Once you complete the specific task, place a checkmark in the "Done" column.

3. *Explain.* If you didn't complete the specific task, write the reason why you didn't in the "Not Done (Reason)" column. This helps you stay accountable to yourself.

Method #2: Dr. Alderson's Modification

Some students prefer a less structured method for organizing their weeks, and I created my own method that you might like to use yourself. It includes the *Weekly Scheduler and Priority List* and a *Today's To Do List.* Complete one Weekly Scheduler and Priority List form at the beginning of each week. Here is how you use it:

1. *Write out goals and priorities.* In the second column, write out your goals and priorities for the week.

2. *Include completion dates.* If there is a completion date, write that date in the third column.

3. *Estimate needed time.* Estimate the total amount of time it will take you to complete the goal.

4. *Estimate time needed per week.* If the goal will take more than a week to finish, calculate the number of hours you will need to work on it each week to complete it.

5. *Prioritize goals.* Now prioritize your goals in the first column.

6. *Commit for the ensuing week.* Lastly, sketch in the last seven columns, representing the days in the coming week, which day(s) you will work on your various goals.

Completed samples of the Weekly Scheduler and Priority List are included in the pages that follow so that you can see exactly how the system looks. The primary purpose of this sheet is to keep you focused on your goals each week, and then to go a step further by committing you to when you will actually work on them.

Complete one of the Today's To Do List forms at the beginning of each day, or the night before. Here is how you use it:

1. Begin by taking items from the Weekly Scheduler and Priority List for that day and writing them in the third column of Today's Do List, along with the time that you specified you would work on them in the fourth column.

2. Write additional items in the third column that you want to accomplish and the time you wish to devote to them in the fourth column.

3. Prioritize the items in the second column.

4. Place a checkmark in the first column once you complete the specified task.

In addition to these steps, there is space near the top of the Today's Do List to include a reward for your priority #1 and #2. Sometimes our highest priorities are things we find difficult, time-consuming, or unpleasant, and if any of these descriptions apply, include a reward that you will give yourself after completing the task.

On Today's To Do List, there is a statement included near the top that says, "Remember: Action Precedes Motivation." This is a reminder to you that interest grows for most of us as a result of becoming proficient at a task. Therefore, motivation generally grows *after* we become good at something.

Lastly, on the bottom of the sheet is space for creating a schedule for that day if you so desire. Sometimes that is helpful if you have a long list of tasks to complete that day. See the sample Today's Do List in the pages that follow so you can see exactly how this works.

SEMESTER TIMETABLE

Week of	Monday	Tuesday	Wednesday	Thursday	Friday
1					
2					
3					
4					
5					
6					
7					
8					
9					
10					
11					
12					
13					
14					
15					
16					

TIME COMMITMENTS SHEET

Scholastic Ability Multiplier
Superior or Gifted x 1
Above Average x 1.5
Average x 2
Below Average x 3

Hours of Lecture Time/Wk.	x	Scholastic Ability Multiplier	=	Hours of Lecture Study
1. _____	x	2. _____	=	3. _____

Hours of Lab + Tutorial + Seminar Time/Wk.	x 1	= Hours of Extra Study
4. _____	x 1	= 5. _____

6. Total Hours of Class Time/wk. (1 + 4)   = _____

7. Total Hours of Academic Work Time/wk. (3 + 5)   = _____

8. Total Hours Committed to School/wk. (6 + 7)   = _____

9. Total Hours of Employment/wk.   = _____

Recommended Maximum Total Hours of Employment
(When Compared to Total Hours Committed to School)

Total Hours Committed to School/wk.	Total Hours of Employment/wk.
41–45 hours	10 hours maximum
36–40 hours	15 hours maximum
31–35 hours	20 hours maximum
26–30 hours	25 hours maximum
21–25 hours	30 hours maximum
16–20 hours	35 hours maximum
11–15 hours	40 hours maximum
10 or less hours	45 hours maximum

WEEKLY TIMETABLE

Time	Monday	Tuesday	Wednesday	Thursday	Friday	Saturday	Sunday
6:30 am							
7:00 am							
7:30 am							
8:00 am							
8:30 am							
9:00 am							
9:30 am							
10:00 am							
10:30 am							
11:00 am							
11:30 am							
12:00 pm							
1:00 pm							
1:30 pm							
2:00 pm							
2:30 pm							
3:00 pm							

	3:30 pm	4:00 pm	4:30 pm	5:00 pm	5:30 pm	6:00 pm	6:30 pm	7:00 pm	7:30 pm	8:00 pm	8:30 pm	9:00 pm	9:30 pm	10:00 pm	10:30 pm	11:00 pm	11:30 pm	12:00 am	12:30 am

ACADEMIC DO LIST

DAY	TASKS	TIME ALLOTTED	DONE	NOT DONE (REASON)
MONDAY				
TUESDAY				
WEDNESDAY				
THURSDAY				
FRIDAY				
SATURDAY				
SUNDAY				

WEEK OF: _____

WEEKLY SCHEDULER AND PRIORITY LIST

PR. #	PRIORITIES AND GOALS	COMPLETION DUE	TOTAL TIME REQ'D	TIME REQ'D PER WEEK	MON.	TUES.	WED.	THUR.	FRI.	SAT.	SUN.

TODAY'S DO LIST

Date: _____

REMEMBER: "Action Precedes Motivation!"

Reward for Priority #1: _____

Reward for Priority #2: _____

DONE	PRIORITY NUMBER	ACCOMPLISH TODAY	TIME REQ'D

SCHEDULE FOR TODAY (OPTIONAL)

7:00–8:00 am _____

8:00–9:00 am _____

9:00–10:00 am _____

10:00–11:00 am _____

11:00–12:00 pm _____

12:00–1:00 pm _____

1:00–2:00 pm _____

2:00–3:00 pm _____

3:00–4:00 pm _____

4:00–5:00 pm _____

5:00–6:00 pm _____

6:00–7:00 pm _____

7:00–8:00 pm _____

8:00–9:00 pm _____

9:00–10:00 pm _____

10:00–11:00 pm _____

WEEK OF: SEPT. 13

WEEKLY SCHEDULER AND PRIORITY LIST SAMPLE

PR. #	PRIORITIES AND GOALS	COMPLETION DUE	TOTAL TIME REQ'D	TIME REQ'D PER WEEK	MON.	TUES.	WED.	THUR.	FRI.	SAT.	SUN.
#2	1. Study for math test.	Sept. 20	6 hours	6	1	1	1		1	1	1
#1	2. Biology assignment.	Sept. 16	5 hours	5	2	3					
#4	3. Serobics workout.	Ongoing	N/A	3	1		1		1		
#3	4. Psychology essay.	Oct. 8	40 hours	10				2		4	4
#5	5. Piano practice.	Ongoing	N/A	4				1	1	1	1

TODAY'S DO LIST EXAMPLE

Date: Monday, Sept. 13

REMEMBER: "Action Precedes Motivation!"

Reward for Priority #1: 20 minutes of jogging

Reward for Priority #2: none

DONE	PRIORITY NUMBER	ACCOMPLISH TODAY	TIME REQ'D
	#2	Study for math test.	1 hour
	#1	Biology assignment.	2 hours
	#3	Aerobics workout.	1 hour
	#6	See my friend, Steve.	1 hour
	#4	Go to the bank.	30 min.
	#5	Housecleaning.	30 min.

SCHEDULE FOR TODAY (OPTIONAL)

7:00–8:00 am *Get up*

8:00–9:00 am *Get to school*

9:00–10:00 am *Biology class*

10:00–11:00 am *English class*

11:00–12:00 pm *Physical Ed.*

12:00–1:00 pm *Lunch*

1:00–2:00 pm *Chemistry class*

2:00–3:00 pm *Go to the bank*

3:00–4:00 pm *Social Studies class*

4:00–5:00 pm *Aerobics class*

5:00–6:00 pm *Go home, eat dinner*

6:00–7:00 pm *Biology assignment*

7:00–8:00 pm *Biology assignment*

8:00–9:00 pm *Study math*

9:00–10:00 pm *Clean room, relax*

10:00–11:00 pm *Go to bed*

No time to see Steve today. Will see him tomorrow.

▶ Self-Hypnosis Applications
Suggestions/Affirmations

(Note: instructions for using suggestions/affirmations are found in Appendix 6.)

1. My motivation will increase toward something as I become more competent.

2. I am becoming increasingly motivated toward important life goals.

3. I am developing a clearer sense of my priorities in life.

4. I persist at important goals even when I don't feel motivated.

5. I work on assignments and goals early by breaking them down into manageable steps.

You might also want to personalize the suggestions/affirmations, as in the following examples:

6. I am becoming motivated to (fill in the blank) _____.

7. I am becoming strongly driven to _____.

8. I can feel my determination to _____ growing stronger and stronger.

9. I am ready to work on _____.

10. There is no better time than NOW!"

[Write some of your own below]:

11.

12.

13.

Imagery

(Note: instructions for using imagery are found in Appendix 5.)

Imagine as clearly as you can the outcome of your goal. For example, for developing an overall motivation toward your career goal, imagine yourself involvd in the career for which you are preparing. See yourself as a happy, content person, and as enjoying most aspects of your employment. Imagine the various aspects of your work in detail. To get an assignment finished (or started), imagine that you are enjoying working on the project, and the relief you will experience once it is finished. You might also imagine the various steps that will be required to get your project underway, and in this way you also build yourself an outline for the assignment.

Script

[CAUTION: *If you have a medical condition or physical problem that might prevent you from doing any of the exercises contained in this script, please use a pencil and cross out the part of the script that contains these exercises. If you are uncertain about whether to exclude something, ask your physician* before *making this self-hypnosis tape*]

"Get comfortable, preferably lying down with your arms and legs uncrossed. Now contract all of your muscles simultaneously, and hold the tension [pause for seven breaths]. Now relax your muscles, and notice the contrast between muscle tension and relaxations [pause for four breaths]. Now contract all of your muscles simultaneously again, and hold the tension [pause for seven breaths]. Now relax your muscles, and notice the contrast once more [pause for four breaths].

"With your eyes open, roll your eyes upward slightly (i.e., toward you forehead) so that you feel a mild eye strain, and then stare at a pot while keeping your eyes in that position. Do not let your gaze drift from that spot. Take five deep abdominal breaths [pause for two breaths]. Inhale the fifth breath extra deep, and while holding it, count backwards mentally, '5-4-3-2-1.' When you get down to '1,' exhale and close your eyes at the same time [pause for two breaths].

"You are becoming increasingly motivated toward important life goals [pause for one breath]. As you focus your energies on your goals, you develop increased competence in what you are doing, and this in turn also increases your motivation as well [pause for one breath]. Regardless of how you feel, you persist in working toward the things that matter most to you [pause for one breath]. You prefer to get down to work early on projects, and it makes you feel good about yourself to do so [pause for two breaths].

"You are developing a clearer sense of your priorities in life and at school [pause for one breath]. Consequently, you work on assignments and goals [pause for one breath]. When you perceive that an assignment or goal is going to be difficult, time-consuming, or unpleasant, you break it down into manageable steps, and you reward yourself for getting each step accomplished [pause for two breaths].

"There is no better time than now to succeed in life and at school [pause for one breath]. This means you are persistent in your efforts, even when adversity tries to hold you back [pause for one breath]. Setbacks may slow you down from time to time, but you are like a bulldozer when it comes to getting the job done [pause for one breath]. You have the stamina to keep pushing forward toward achieving the goals you have set for yourself [pause for one breath]. You are ready to get down to work [pause for one breath]. Your determination is impenetrable [pause for one breath]. Like an Eveready Battery, you keep going [pause for one breath] and going [pause for one breath] and going [pause for two breaths].

"When you are ready to leave self-hypnosis, first silently tell yourself that you will count to five and that at the count of five, you will come out of self-hypnosis feeling refreshed, relaxed, and confident. Then awaken yourself by counting to five mentally, and say, 'AWAKE!' to yourself [pause for three breaths]. Then open your eyes."

▶ Summary

This chapter has shown you how to persist toward the goals that matter to you. By following the techniques outlined in the conventional methods section, you will also avoid procrastination and become well-organized for school. The self-hypnosis applications will assist you in building the kind of impenetrable determination that characterizes highly successful individuals.

Chapter Seven

The Fourth Power: Balance

"All things in moderation, nothing in excess."

Greek proverb

When my two children were both young, I remember a year when I worked myself to the bone. Starting in September, I was a full-time employee at a community college. I saw up to ten clients a week for hypnotherapy, one out of every three weekends I worked in a residential treatment program Fridays from 4:00 pm until Sundays at 4:00 pm, and when I wasn't working I was so exhausted that I drank whisky and beer. My stomach grew as my spirits sank so that by May, I was so depressed I thought that I was going to die. I could hardly function anymore, and I had lost all desire to do anything but pout. It took me the next four months and a psychiatrist who told me that I might do better if I looked after myself to get back on my feet again. I've never forgotten the psychiatrist's words ever since.

Have you ever tried to accomplish too many at the same time?

Do you remember how you felt as you struggled to keep your head above water, yet the tides of pressure keep trying to drag you back down? To be successful in life, you have to remember that balance is absolutely necessary. You only have limited time and energy, and how you spend them is crucially important.

If all of your time and energy are being devoted to school and/or work, the rest of your life suffers. If all of your time and energy are being devoted to play, school and/or work suffers. *Balance* means that you invest sufficient amounts of time in the various domains. Optimal health requires balance in the following areas of life:

- educational/academic and/or work and career (i.e., the work side of life),
- leisure and recreational (i.e., enjoying free time),
- social time(i.e., spending time with others, and having significant relationships with them),
- physical needs (i.e., exercise, sleep, diet, rest, and relaxation),
- spiritual needs(i.e., finding purpose and meaning in life).

If your life remains unbalanced for an extended period, you will likely experience exhaustion and perhaps even feel immobilized in all domains of life. A completely burnt-out student, for example, feels too tired to take part in most activities, including studying, concentrating, thinking, and writing. As a psychologist, I have seen far too many students who have become so burnt-out that they needed to withdraw from one or more classes. In severe cases, these students have needed to withdraw from the entire semester.

You can become burnt-out when the load you are carrying is either uneven (i.e., *breadth*), meaning that one or more areas of your life has been ignored over a significant period of time, or when the load is overwhelming (i.e., *depth*) in one or more areas of your life. A problem of breadth would eventually occur if you ignored or avoided one or more of the life domains. For example, if you focused your time and energies on the first four domains listed above, but ignored or avoided the spiritual domain, you could easily become self-centered and passionless. If you neglected the physical domain, your physical health would deteriorate.

A problem of depth would eventually occur if too much of your time and energy were being devoted to one life domain. Sometimes this occurrence is unavoidable. For example, if you are a star athlete and you are in the middle of game season, you may have little time to devote to school and family responsibilities. Alternatively, if you are in the middle of final exams, you may have little time to devote to the domain of leisure and recreation. These examples pose little problem for most students because the duration is short. Problems of depth can develop when the duration of imbalances becomes longer term.

It is also important to find the path of moderation, especially in the physical domain. Students in colleges and universities are well known for alcohol and drug use, and occasionally abuse those substances as well. This is a difficult area for most of us to assess on our own because if our friends are heavy substance users, we may not think anything of it when we engage in the same abuse. It is beyond the scope of this book to review substance abuse and its management. If you suspect you may be developing a problem in this area, please seek out counseling services at your school.

Moderation must also be maintained found in the other components comprising the physical domain. This means avoiding under- and overindulgence in eating, sleeping, and exercising. Too little or too much of any of these activities is unhealthy.

In this chapter, I will review some ways to help you maintain a balance most of the time. This is not always possible in the short run because despite our efforts to stay balanced, unforeseen circumstances occur. If someone in your immediate family became gravely ill, for example, your attention would be temporarily drawn away from maintaining your personal balance. The important thing is to regain balance as soon as it once again becomes possible to do so.

▶ Conventional Methods of Fostering Balance
Assess Where You Are and Where You Want to Be

Complete the questionnaire below periodically to assess and reassess where you are at in your attempts to balance your life. If you need or want to make a change within any of the five domains to attain better balance, either place a checkmark in the + column; place a checkmark in the—column if you want to do less of something in that domain. In the last column, write out specifically what you intend to do differently.

For example, if you need to get more exercise, write down exactly what you intend to do (e.g., *Ride exercise bike for 20 minutes, three times a week*, or *Lift weights for 60 minutes, four times a week*).

	Domain	+	-	What will you do differently? Be precise.
1	School/Work			
2	Leisure/Recreation			
3	Social			
4	Physical			
5	Spiritual			

Stick to It

Once you have decided what you need to do differently, you need ways to help you stick to your plans. Lifestyles tend to be very habitual; we keep doing things the way we always did them. To break the cycle, write down your plans on the forms contained in Chapter 6 (i.e., the forms designed to help you organize your time—either on the Weekly Timetable Sheet or on the Weekly Schedule and Priority List). If you anticipate that getting down to doing it will be a struggle for you, be sure you build in rewards for successful achievement (Chapter 6 also explains how to use rewards).

Commit to a Friend, or Join Them

It is often easier to stick to a goal if we commit ourselves by telling someone else about the goal. Part of the reason this helps is that it offers us social support, and part of the reason is that it makes us accountable. Once we make a verbal or written commitment to another person, we feel that we need to live up to our words.

It is even more helpful if you can find someone who also wants to work toward the same goal with you. If you want to work out regularly, for example, having a work out partner is very helpful. If you can't find someone else to do the activity with, consider joining a group that partakes in the activity. For example, if you want to lose weight, there are many weight loss programs (e.g., *Weight Watchers*) that can help you achieve your goal. If you want to get fit, most commercial gyms have aerobics classes available.

▶ Self-Hypnosis Applications
Suggestions/Affirmations

(Note: instructions for using suggestions/affirmations are found in Appendix 6.)

1. I am striving to find a healthy balance in my life.

2. Like brushing my teeth, exercise, nutritional eating, and adequate rest and sleep are also part of my daily rituals.

3. When I have too many competing interests, I prioritize and let go of the lesser goals, at least temporarily.

4. When I need to, I am okay with saying "no" to people's demands, including my own.

5. I strive for moderation in all things that can affect my health.

[Write some of your own below]:

6.

7.

8.

Imagery
(Note: instructions for using imagery are found in Appendix 5.)

Visualizations for the Deficient Dimension
If you have decided that you need to do more of something in order to have better balance in your life, spend time visualizing yourself doing more of the activities that will help you attain balance. If you think you should get out dancing more with your friends, picture yourself going out with them and dancing to your heart's content. Also imagine how much fun you would be having.

During times in your life when you cannot balance your life because of circumstances beyond your control, you can also use this type of imagery as a way to help offset the lack of balance. If you need a holiday, imagining yourself on a beach in great detail can imitate the actual experience to some extent. If you had to stop working out because of an injury, continuing to imagine your workouts will help keep the mental discipline needed so that you can more readily return to working out once you recover.

Visualizations for the Excessive Dimension
If you have decided that you need to do less of something in order to have better balance in your life, imagine ways you can reduce the amount of time spent in the activity or the intensity of involvement in the activity. For example, let's say you have decided to drink less when you go out with friends. Imagine ways you can reduce the amount you drink. Here are some possible images:

• having a glass or two of water after each alcoholic beverage,
• deciding to be the designated driver every second time you go out with friends,
• asking your friends to cut you off after a set number of drinks,
• switching to a lower alcohol content drink (e.g., light beer instead of regular beer).

Also, imagine how much better you will feel the next day.

If your goal is to eat less calorie-rich foods and thereby lose weight, picture yourself eating healthy foods and enjoying them. Also visualize yourself as a slimmer person—how will you look once you have lost the excess weight? Another helpful image is to see yourself getting an appropriate amount of exercise.

Script

[CAUTION: *If you have a medical condition or physical problem that might prevent you from doing any of the exercises contained in this script, please use a pencil and cross out the part of the script that contains these exercises. If you are uncertain about whether to exclude something, ask your physician* before *making this self-hypnosis tape*]

"Get comfortable, preferably lying down with your arms and legs uncrossed. Now contract all of your muscles simultaneously, and hold the tension [pause for seven breaths]. Now relax your muscles, and notice the contrast between muscle tension and relaxation [pause for four breaths]. Now contract all of your muscles simultaneously again, and hold the tension [pause for seven breaths]. Now relax your muscles, and notice the contrast once more [pause for four breaths].

"With your eyes open, roll your eyes upward slightly (i.e., toward your forehead) so that you feel a mild eye strain, and then stare at a spot while keeping your eyes in that position. Do not let your gaze drift from that spot. Take five deep abdominal breaths [pause for two breaths]. Inhale the fifth breath extra deep, and while holding it, count backwards mentally '5-4-3-2-1.' When you get down to '1,' exhale and close your eyes at the same time [pause for two breaths].

"You are striving to find a healthy balance in your life. You are committed to spending time focused on the five domains of life: school and/or work, leisure and recreation, social, physical, and spiritual. You know that school is demanding, and when you are working hard, you know that you also need to take care of your physical needs. It is no wonder you feel a strong desire to get adequate exercise, sufficient sleep, proper diet, and enough rest and relaxation [pause for two breaths].

"When faced with too many commitments or obligations, you prioritize these and let go or suspend temporarily the ones of lesser importance [pause for one breath]. You know that you cannot do everything at once, and you are forgiving of yourself when you need to put some things off for a time [pause for one breath]. When the load is too great, you are okay with saying 'no' to people's demands [pause for two breaths].

"You strive for moderation in all things that affect your health [pause for one breath]. You are aware of what you are doing that is good for you, and you are aware of what you are doing that is not [pause for one breath]. Because you love yourself deeply, you take the necessary steps to let go or at least minimize unhealthy activities [pause for one breath]. This is your body, and you are committed to looking after it [pause for two breaths].

"When you are ready to leave self-hypnosis, first silently tell yourself that you will count to five and that at the count of five, you will come out of self-hypnosis feeling refreshed, relaxed, and confident. Then awaken yourself by counting to five mentally, and say, 'AWAKE!' to yourself [pause for 3 breaths]. Then open your eyes."

▶ Summary

This chapter reviewed the fourth power of success: balance. You can become burnt out when the load you are carrying is either uneven (i.e., *breadth*) or when the load is overwhelming (i.e., *depth*) in one or more areas. Optimal health requires balance, and this can be attained when the issues of depth and breadth across the five domains of life are addressed. You also need to find the path of moderation in those activities that can affect your physical health.

This chapter ends Part II of this book. In Part III, applications of self-hypnosis to specific academic challenges are presented, including (1) learning and studying, (2) exam anxiety, (3) writer's block, (4) speech anxiety, and (5) career exploration.

Part III

Other Powerful Applications

Chapter Eight

Turning the Inner Keys to Learning and Studying

Leslie has found it difficult to retain what she is trying to learn. When she is about to study, she gets herself ready by turning on the radio to the dance music station before she lays out her books on her bed. While reading, she chews gum and bops her head to the music. Her concentration is unfocused and her reading is periodically interrupted by thoughts about the music and thoughts about her boyfriend. Nonetheless, she assumes that she knows the material quite well after reading it over three times. The next day Leslie writes her midterm in social studies. She is shocked that she cannot remember three quarters of the answers to the questions. She feels devastated when her exam is returned to her with a mark of 39 percent.

Obviously self-hypnosis is not a panacea for everything. The most effective students, regardless of whether they use self-hypnosis as an adjunct to their success, need to do two things:
1. Dedicate *sufficient time* to school.
2. Use *effective study techniques*.

Chapter 6 covered determining how much time you need to study and getting motivated to do so. Please review that chapter if needed. This chapter will look at tips you can use to improve your concentration, your memory, and your study skills.

▶ Conventional Methods of Learning and Studying
Improve Your Concentration

Creating a Learning Environment

You need to create an environment that is conducive to learning. This means eliminating unnecessary distractions. As we associate bed with sleep, studying in bed is not recommended. Instead, pick a desk preferably in a quiet non-distracting location in the house, or pick a table as your second best option. If you want music in the background, play baroque music—it has been shown to enhance concentration (Bancroft, 1976). Baroque music is a definable type of classical music written between 1700 and 1750 ("Welcome to the wonderful world," n.d.). It is both lively and soothing at the same time. Some of the famous composers of the baroque period include Antonio Vivaldi, George Frideric Handel, and Johann Sebastian Bach.

Shaping Your Skill at Concentrating

When you sit down to read or study, work on your materials until you begin to find your concentration drifting. The moment this occurs, stop working and write down how long it took before your concentration diminished. Let's say you lasted ten minutes. Take a short break and then return to your study, but attempt to increase the amount of time you can concentrate before your attention drifts during the next sitting. If needed, add rewards to increase your study time (see Chapter 6 for a discussion about using rewards). Incrementally, then, you increase your concentration time in this way until you can stay focused for up to forty-five minutes or so. Few people can continue concentrating without a break beyond the forty-five--minute mark.

Improve Your Memory

The least efficient means of learning something is to learn by rote, which is trying to remember something by sheer repetition. For example, if you are trying to remember someone's name and you simply repeat it to yourself 100 times, you are learning by rote. It may shock you when you see that person two weeks later, and alas, you have forgotten her name already!

The key to improving memory is to process information on a deeper level (Craik & Lockhart, 1972). If instead of learning by rote, you processed the name at a deeper level, your ability to remember it would be enhanced. For example, if the woman's name was Jane and if she had long hair, you might associate her name with Jane from the Tarzan novel. The mere fact of making this association greatly increases the likelihood you will remember her name. When you see her next time, you now have a number of ways by which to access her name from your memory, including recalling it via (a) rote (you likely repeated her name to yourself a number of times); (b) the name Jane because of its association with Tarzan; (c) the name Tarzan first, and then its association with Jane; (d) association between her long hair and the name Jane; or (e) some combination of these memory cues.

There are a number of methods to help you process information more deeply, the most common of which are called mnemonic devices. *Mnemonic devices* are various methods of organizing material so that the material becomes easier to recall later (Oracle Education Foundation, n.d.). There are several mnemonic devices that have been developed, and the following are the most typical:

- acronyms and acrostics,
- rhymes,
- chunking,
- imagery,
- the method of Loci.

Acronyms and Acrostics

Acronyms result when we combine letters where each letter acts as a cue to something we wish to remember. For example, a common acronym used for remembering the correct order of the colors of the rainbow (e.g., red, orange, yellow, green, blue, indigo, and violet) is the name, ROY G. BIV.

An acrostic is when we create a phrase or sentence based on the first or last letter of each word of a list that we wish to remember. To remember the correct order of the planets around our solar system (e.g., Mercury, Venus, Earth, Mars, Jupiter, Saturn, Uranus, Neptune, and Pluto), a common acrostic is "My Very Earnest Mother Just Served Us Nine Pickles" (or substitute the word "pizzas" for "pickles").

Rhymes

Using rhymes to help you remember entails creating sayings that have similar sounds at the end of each line. For example, "In fourteen hundred and ninety-two, Columbus sailed the ocean blue," or "'i' before 'e' except after 'c.'"

Chunking

Chunking involves putting information into categories, or *chunks*, which help you to remember. For example, if you had to remember a list of unrelated letters, such as TWANBACBSCPR-CIA, at first glance this would be a difficult. By chunking the letters together as follows, TWA NBA CBS CPR CIA, it would become much easier as each of these chunks represents a well-known abbreviation.

Imagery

Imagery can be used to memorize word pairs. If you needed to remember the word pair, "dog-flies," you could picture a dog irritated by hundreds of flies hovering around it and landing on it. The more dramatic or surprising the visual image, the better retained it usually becomes.

The Method of Loci
The method of Loci dates back to Ancient Greece. To use the method, you need to imagine a place that you know quite well so that you can visualize several locations within it. Then you associate each bit of information you want to remember with a location within that familiar place.

For example, let's imagine that you need to remember a list of items to purchase at the grocery store (your list includes bananas, peanut butter, olives, cheese spread, watermelon, canned tuna, chicken, and ice cream), and you are going to associate each item with locations within your bedroom. This is how it might look:

1. I walk in my bedroom holding a *banana*.

2. As I enter the room, I go to my desk and find *peanut butter* smeared across the top of it.

3. On top of my computer keyboard are *olives* resting between the keys.

4. I look up at my computer screen and find it is covered with *cheese spread*.

5. I go to the closet and find *watermelons* in the way.

6. Once inside, I notice someone has put *cans of tuna* between my jeans.

7. I flop on my bed in frustration and my head lands on *raw chicken*.

8. I am just about to scream when mom enters my room eating *ice cream*.

Once you make the associations a few times in your head, you are ready to go to the grocery store. There, you remember the items in order by remembering the above sequence, beginning with you entering your bedroom and concluding with your mom entering it.

Improve Your Studying and Notetaking

Would you be interested in a combined study and notetaking method that offers the following advantages?

• provides you feedback as to exactly how much you know

(e.g., if you can thoroughly answer eight out of ten questions, you know your retention rate is 80 percent),

• reduces exam anxiety because of this feedback mechanism (i.e., confidence and exam anxiety are inversely related, which means that as your confidence increases for what you have learned, your exam anxiety diminishes),

• builds in processing of material to a deeper level, thus facilitating memory enhancement,

• structures your notes in an efficient manner, thus permitting easier studying.

A modified form of the famous SQ4R method [i.e., **Survey, Question, Read,** "**Rite**" (write), **Recite, Review**) will provide these advantages for you. Here is how it works:

1. Set up all of your notepaper—both for lectures and for taking notes from your text and other readings—by adding a margin two-and-a-half inches to three inches from the left side of each page.

2. In lectures, write your notes only on the right side of your notepaper.

3. In a sense, your notes are like answers to questions or problems. As soon as possible after the lecture, review your notes and make up questions that your notes are answering. Write these questions to the left of your margin.

4. Now your lecture notes are set up in a "question-answer" format. When you are ready to study, simply cover up the right hand side of each page, ask yourself the questions on the left side, and recite back the content of your covered notes. If you miss any points, spend more time memorizing this material.

5. If you can recall your answers to questions on three different occasions without having to check your notes, you have studied the material enough. A quick review before the exam is still a must, however.

6. On the next page is a sample of this form of notetaking. The sample also includes instructions for using SQ4R to take notes from your text or other readings.

Sometimes you will decide that you don't need to take notes from what you are about to read and study. This is generally *not* recommended, but there are occasions when the material is very easy or you don't have the time to do a thorough job. If you are not intending to take notes from what you read, the order of SQ4R should be modified. Here is how it would then look:

1. *Survey.* The scanning that you do during the survey stage provides you with an overview of what the chapter is about. Flip through the pages, scanning the headings and sub-headings, note drawings, graphs, and pictures, and read the chapter summary.

2. *Question.* Turn headings and sub-headings into questions, and form other questions as you begin reading.

3. *Read.* As you begin reading, look for the answers to the questions you first raised. Use underlining and checkmarks beside important points in pencil, and highlight as well.

4. *Recite.* When you have finished reading a small section, look away from your book and briefly recite the answer(s) to your questions (or ask yourself questions about what you have just read, and summarize it in your own words).

5. *Relate.* Remembering material that is personally meaningful is easier, and as you read a section, try to link new facts and concepts with information you already know.

6. *Review.* When you're done reading, skim back over the chapter. Check your memory by reciting and quizzing yourself on different occasions. Make frequent review a part of your study habits.

THE "SQ4R" STUDY METHOD

What is the best way to set up my lecture notes?

Set up your lecture notes by placing a margin two-and-a-half to three inches from the left side of each page. As you take notes in lecture, keep all of them on the right hand side of the page, adding questions later on the left side.

What is the best way to set up my text-book notes?

Use the same format, and follow the instructions below:

What is the most effective study method?

"SQ4R"

What are the six stages in this method for textbook reading and studying?

1. *Survey*. Flip through the pages, scanning the headings and sub-headings, note drawings, graphs, and pictures, and read the chapter summary.

2. *Question*. Turn headings and sub-headings into questions, and form other questions as you begin your *first* reading.

3. *Read*. First reading—place checkmarks beside important points in pencil (do *not* highlight at this stage).

4. *Rite ("write")*. As you begin your second reading, write out questions in the left column of your notepaper as you come up to each sub-heading or sec-

tion. Write answers to these questions in the column of your notepaper (i.e., like this example) in…
a) *your own words,*
b) *using abbreviations,*
c) *from memory initially.*
As you read the section, complete your answers (add to them), and add further questions and answers as needed. If you highlight your texts, do this during this your second reading.

5. *Recite*. This has already occurred for the first time while you prepared your notes (remember having recited answers by recalling them from memory). Before leaving your study session, cover the right fhand side, and attempt to recite your answers to the questions on the left side of the page.

6. *Review*. Periodically review your notes through this process of recitation (step #5). When you can recall your answers to questions on three different occasions without having to check your notes, you have studied the material enough. A quick review before the exam is still a must.

▶ Self-Hypnosis Applications
Improve Your Concentration

One of the simplest methods of improving concentration, called the *concentrate and recall exercise,* was developed by Porter (1978). As you get yourself ready to study with the materials in front of you, briefly pause and say three times firmly and slowly to yourself, "concentrate and recall." This will help to focus your attention.

Two other helpful exercises were developed by Porter (1978). The *relax/let go exercise* was intended to reduce tension that develops during a study period. Take five slow deep breaths, and think at the same time to *relax* as you breathe in and to *let go* as you breathe out. You can use this technique at any time without others being aware.

The last technique Porter (1978) called the *REC/TTF exercise,* and it is used for reducing tiredness and fear. As in the preceding exercise, concentrate on the words, "relaxation, energy, and confidence" (REC) as you breathe in, and "tension, tiredness, and fear" (TTF) as you breathe out. Anywhere from five to ten breaths is recommended.

Improve Your Memory

The best advice I have read about memory enhancement is from Kihlstrom and Barnhardt (1993):

> We can remember things better by paying active attention to them at the time they occur, deliberately engaging in elaborative and organizational activity that will establish links between one item of information and another; and we can facilitate forgetting by neglecting to do so. Forgetting will increase with the passage of time, if we allow it to happen; but continued rumination about the to-be-forgotten material may prevent this natural process from occurring. Once-forgotten items can be recovered, too, if somehow we are able to find the right cues to gain access to them; and

some spontaneous recovery is to be expected as well, especially if the information was well encoded in the first place... In the absence of conscious recollection, sheer guessing—influenced by implicit memory, which is much less constrained by the conditions of encoding and retrieval—may lead the person to better-than-chance levels of memory performance (p. 115).

Memory enhancement through hypnosis and self-hypnosis is highly debated and the results of studies are equivocal, meaning that some studies conclude that hypnosis can facilitate memory while other studies find the opposite result. An excellent review of the use of hypnosis in criminal investigations did conclude, however, that if the information to be retained "is personally relevant and emotional, hypnotic techniques appear to possess definite potential to enhance recall to a mild or moderate degree in some individuals, without necessarily including an increase in inaccuracies or false recollections" (Brown, Scheeflin, & Hammond, 1998, p. 352).

Given that some memory enhancement may occur for some people through the use of self-hypnosis, some of these techniques are included in the suggestions/affirmations, imagery, and script sections that follow.

Improve Your Studying
The Sandwich Method
Arons and Bubeck (1971) created the *sandwich method* of studying, which offers some advantages to students:
- promotes the proper attitude and atmosphere for studying (helps to get you focused and "in the mood" for studying),
- reduces anxiety, thereby assisting in improving your concentration,
- produces a positive mindset and positive expectancy for desirable results.

Here is how you use the sandwich method:

1. *Get ready.* Prepare study materials.

2. *Read suggestion 1.* From a prepared card read suggestion #1 five times, then drop the card.

3. Suggestion 1: *"The material I am about to study will be deeply impressed and permanently retained."*

4. *Hypnotize yourself.* Put yourself into self-hypnosis for three minutes using the basic induction (Appendix 2).

5. *Study.* Study for a short period—stop before you are tired.

6. *Read suggestion 2.* From a prepared card read suggestion #2 five times, then drop the card.

7. Suggestion 2: *"The material I have just studied is permanently retained and is easily available when I require it."*

8. *Re-hypnotize yourself.* Put yourself into self-hypnosis for three minutes.

9. *Repeat.* Return to step 4 above, and continue studying.

10. *Optional.* After step 6 above, relax with something completely different—sports, TV, music, etcetera for five minutes. Then repeat steps 2 through 8 until study is completed.

The Blackboard Method

Another technique for studying is using Shrader's *blackboard method* (cited in Cohen, 1982). Here is how you use the method:

1. *Hypnotize yourself.* Put yourself into self-hypnosis using the basic induction (Appendix 2).

2. *Visualize a blackboard.* Visualize a mythical blackboard and write the information on the blackboard that you are studying.

The above method has been found to be helpful for memorizing mathematical and scientific formulas specifically, but the method holds promise for studying other materials as well.

One of my methods involves reading the material you intend to learn onto a cassette tape, and then listening to the tape while in self-hypnosis. Give yourself a few minutes lead time at the beginning of the tape to get yourself into a calm state of self-hypnosis. Such a method might be useful in learning material that would ordinarily be learned by rote (e.g., straight facts or definitions). Be sure you spend time reciting the material that you heard after the tape ends to ensure that you have learned it.

Suggestions/Affirmations

(Note: instructions for using suggestions/affirmations are found in Appendix 6.)

For Improved Concentration

1. My concentration for study is improving.
2. When I sit down to study, I can concentrate for increasing periods of time.
3. I am becoming more focused on my studies.
4. I am becoming more interested in what I am learning about.
5. My mind is clear and efficient.

[Write some of your own below]:

6.

7.

8.

For Improved Memory

1. My memory is improving.
2. My ability to learn new information is getting better and better.
3. Because of my improved study methods, I can easily recall information when I want to.
4. I can access information from my memory quickly and effectively.
5. My memory works like a high-speed computer.

[Write some of your own below]:

6.

7.

8.

For Improved Studying

1. I feel motivated to study.

2. When I sit down to study, I completely focus on what is in front of me.

3. I am conditioning myself to study for longer periods of time.

4. I feel confident in my ability to learn.

5. I review my material periodically, reciting out loud or silently that which I have learned.

[Write some of your own below]:

6.

7.

8.

Imagery

(Note: instructions for using imagery are found in Appendix 5.)

For Improved Concentration

Imagine yourself approaching your study area, sitting down, and focusing with deep concentration on your study materials. Picture each aspect of this scene in great detail. Also visualize yourself studying for longer periods of time before needing to take a break.

For Improved Memory

Imagine that all of your notes are set up as described earlier (i.e., in a question-answer format). Now picture yourself covering up the right hand side of each page and finding that you can recall the covered information quite well. Feel the growing sense of confidence as you find you can answer most of the questions this way without needing to review the covered information much at all.

For Improved Studying

The best image here is to imagine yourself using the SQ4R method of studying consistently. Imagine yourself opening your textbook or other study material and going through each of the six stages of SQ4R [i.e., **Survey, Question, Read, "Rite"** (write),

Recite, Review]. It also helps if you can create a feeling of enjoyment while you go through this image.

Script

[CAUTION: *If you have a medical condition or physical problem that might prevent you from doing any of the exercises contained in this script, please use a pencil and cross out the part of the script that contains these exercises. If you are uncertain about whether to exclude something, ask your physician* before *making this self-hypnosis tape*]

"Get comfortable, preferably lying down with your arms and legs uncrossed. Now contract all of your muscles simultaneously, and hold the tension [pause for seven breaths]. Now relax your muscles, and notice the contrast between muscle tension and relaxation [pause for four breaths]. Now contract all of your muscles simultaneously again, and hold the tension [pause for seven breaths]. Now relax your muscles, and notice the contrast once more [pause for four breaths].

"With your eyes open, roll your eyes upward slightly (i.e., toward your forehead so that you feel a mild eye strain, and then stare at a spot while keeping your eyes in that position. Do not let your gaze drift from that spot. Take five deep abdominal breaths [pause for two breaths]. Inhale the fifth breath extra deep, and while holding it, count backwards mentally, '5-4-3-2-1.' When you get down to '1,' exhale and close your eyes at the same time [pause for two breaths].

"Your concentration for reading and studying is constantly improving [pause for one breath]. When you sit down to read or study, you can concentrate for longer periods of time [pause for one breath]. For whatever reason, you are becoming more focused and more interested in what you are learning about [pause for one breath]. Your mind is clear and it works efficiently [pause for two breaths].

"Your memory is also steadily improving [pause for one breath]. Your ability to learn new information is getting better and better [pause for one breath]. Because of your improved study methods, you can easily recall information whenever you want to [pause for one breath]. Your mind works like a high-speed computer [pause for one breath]—you retain that which you input, and you remember that which is needed for output [pause for two breaths].

"You find it interesting how your motivation to study is growing [pause for one breath]. Your goals are important to you, and achieving good or exceptional grades in school will help you immensely [pause for one breath]. Part of the exercise is learning to be well disciplined in life, so you know that all of the studying is serving you well [pause for one breath]. You feel confident in your ability to learn [pause for one breath]. You review your material periodically, reciting out loud or silently that which you have learned [pause for two breaths].

"When you are ready to leave self-hypnosis, first silently tell yourself that you will count to five and that at the count of five, you will come out of self-hypnosis feeling refreshed, relaxed, and confident. Then awaken yourself by counting to five mentally, and say, 'AWAKE!' to yourself [pause for three breaths]. Then open your eyes."

▶ Summary

This chapter has shown you how to improve your ability to learn new material. It has focused on improving your concentration, improving your memory, and improving your studying and notetaking behaviour. Consequently, you will soon be enjoying better grades without having to work as hard as you imagined. Studying will soon become something you enjoy instead of something you have to endure.

Chapter Nine

Taking the Terror Out of Tests

"Perhaps the only thing more painful than this is a slow death," Richard thought as he sat down to write his final exam. He noticed his hands were cold and clammy, trembling. He also noticed his shakiness resided deep within himself. He looked at the first question and, like Brainfreeze from a 7-Eleven Slurpee, his mind drew a blank. Hours of study didn't seem to matter now. Most of the questions looked easy enough, yet answers were not forthcoming. By the end of the test, Richard felt so demoralized and so stupid, he couldn't rush out of the classroom fast enough before breaking into tears.

A week later, the exam was returned, and looking over the questions now he felt as though he were looking at a different test than the one he wrote. How could he have missed even the easy questions? Richard knew his material—what went wrong?

Likely this is not a topic that you need an introduction to—you have already experienced it. Every serious student will feel some degree of anxiety before and during an exam. When this anxiety is mild-to-moderate, it acts to create a positive excitement and feeling of challenge. In turn, this helps you to work quickly under the pressure of time constraints. When anxiety becomes severe-to-incapacitating, it shuts down your ability to think clearly.

> Research has shown that there is a *negative correlation* between the levels of anxiety that students have and their test scores. In other words, the more anxious you become, the lower your test score will probably be... Anxiety also hurts your self-confidence—and low self-confidence can contribute to low test scores. (Johnson, 1997, p.1).

Exam anxiety is the self-inflicted punishment for either not feeling capable or for having unrealistic expectations. Exam anxiety is "self-inflicted" because no one is causing the reaction, other than yourself. Regarding *capability*, people of at least average intelligence are capable of doing well in most programs at college and university. However, many people do not *feel* capable because of self-defeating thoughts and beliefs that are deeply ingrained. These thoughts often lead to students making insufficient effort, which in turn becomes a self-fulfilling prophecy (i.e., students neglecting to study because they don't feel capable, and then failing because they didn't study).

If you haven't prepared adequately for an exam, you will end up feeling threatened and uptight. "Cramming" the night before a test will probably leave you feeling tense, which leads to disturbed sleep. The only remedy for this type of anxiety is getting down to work early enough to avoid this pitfall. Good study habits are essential if you wish to avoid exam anxiety.

Regarding *unrealistic expectations*, there are individuals whose expectations are far greater than what is considered reasonable. For example, if you have not attended classes for fifteen years and you have now returned to school, it would be unrealistic to expect that you would be an A student in your first year. Becoming an accomplished student takes time. You need to be able to master your studies and your time to pull off A's consistently, not to mention you must a have high aptitude for all of your subjects.

Furthermore, when you have unrealistic expectations, the emphasis switches from "learning" to "performance." If studying is done for the sole purpose of grades, a tremendous performance pressure ensues. This pressure becomes exam anxiety. It is important to study for the purpose of learning. If learning is emphasized, instead of grades, the exam situation becomes an opportunity to communicate what you have learned. Good grades will follow naturally if you have learned the material. This type of exam anxiety is created by perception, but it is clear from the following example that perception can affect our emotions substantially.

If you tell yourself thoughts such as, "I *must* get an A on this exam," or "This is a do or die situation—if I fail this test, it proves I am stupid and worthless," then you are going to turn an exam into a *threat* situation. Compare these beliefs to thoughts like, "I know this material *very* well, and I have every reason to believe that I will succeed," or "I am going to stay calm because all I can do is my best anyway," or, "If I fail, I can handle it. I will learn from my failures as well as my successes, making it likely that I will succeed the majority of the time." With these beliefs, you will likely see the exam as a *challenge*, and view it positively and confidently. Begin to feed your mind positive thoughts on a regular basis.

Be aware that the goal of becoming a successful student is not to eliminate exam anxiety. Instead, the intent is to reduce it to a point where you are alert and functioning at a high intellectual capacity. Most of us accomplish tasks better when we feel some degree of excitement (which you may label as mild to moderate anxiety). If you are too relaxed, you simply won't work at peak efficiency.

▶ Conventional Methods of Reducing Exam Anxiety

Assess the Problem

If you suffer exam anxiety, the first thing is to do is to conduct a careful assessment of what is causing it. Turn to Appendix 9 and complete the questionnaire there to help you make this determination. If you have not learned how to manage your time—and therefore do not study enough—or if you have not learned how to study properly, be sure you pay special attention to Chapters 6 and 8, respectively.

Writing an exam provides you with an invaluable opportunity to gain feedback regarding your learning and your performance. When you get the test back, go over it carefully to extract the reasons why you didn't get 100 percent on it. Ask yourself the following questions:

1. Did I study the wrong material? How can I find out what to study for the next exam?

2. What types of questions threw me off—e.g., multiple choice, short answer, essay? How can I modify my study approach for the types of questions I have trouble answering?

3. Was the exam itself constructed in a fair manner? If not, what can I do to prepare for this type of test the next time?

4. What are the gaps in my knowledge for this subject? How can I make up these deficiencies?

Reduce Exam Anxiety

The following psychological methods have proven themselves helpful in reducing excessive exam anxiety:

1. Relaxation Techniques,

2. Cognitive Therapy,

3. Systematic Desensitization Therapy,

4. Imagery (as imagery is a self-hypnotic technique, it will be covered in the next section).

Relaxation Techniques

Why learn to relax? Relaxation is the opposite of anxiety, so by learning to relax, you can learn to release tension whenever and wherever you choose. You will find relaxation methods in Appendices 2, 5, and 7.

Cognitive Therapy

We reviewed the triple-column technique in Chapter 4, and the instructions are repeated below applied to exam anxiety:

MALADAPTIVE THOUGHT OR BELIEF	QUESTIONING IT	HEALTHY THOUGHT OR BELIEF
"I am no good at math, and I am going to fail the exam."	"Okay, math is difficult for me, but what proof do I have that I cannot pass a test in it if I work hard enough? Past failures do not dictate my entire future as a student."	"If I dedicate more time to learning math, I will be able to pass the next exam. I don't have to get an A in it. I just need to get through it—and learn."

This is how you use the triple-column:

1. *Brainstorm your thoughts.*In the first column write out the thought(s) or belief(s) causing your anxiety. You might already be aware of some of these thoughts, in which case you can record them now. Another approach is to wait until something triggers you to feel anxious before making an entry.

2. *Challenge yourself.* In the second column, challenge the logic behind the thought or belief. Use the questions below to help you do this:

a) What proof do I have that this is true?

b) Do I have any evidence that indicates it is not true?

c) Are there any competing "truths?" Is another belief just as valid?

d) Does everyone think this way? Why not?

e) Does agreeing with the majority on this make it necessarily correct?

f) Where did I learn this message? Is it possible that the messenger was wrong?

g) What purpose is served in continuing to believe this?

h) What price do I pay for continuing to believe this?

i) What will be the advantages of believing something different?

j) Are my feelings about this providing an accurate gauge of what I should believe?

k) If I was helping someone else deal with this, what would I want him to believe?

l) If I knew I would be dead tomorrow, would I be happy believing this?

Once you have challenged your thinking, write out the challenge in the second column.

3. *Turn things around.* In the third column, write out a healthy version of the thought(s) or belief(s) that you would like to substitute for the one written in the first column.

4. *Focus on the third column.* Spend time focusing on the thought(s) or belief(s) written in the third column. The more you

absorb yourself in repeating the thought(s) or belief(s) in column three, the more you will internalize the message.

5. *Repeat when necessary.* Whenever you catch yourself repeating similar anxious thoughts to yourself, either write them down again and repeat steps 2 through 5, or do the work in your head by talking to yourself, either silently or out loud. Remember to do both the challenge and then to substitute the healthy thought or belief.

Systematic Desensitization Therapy

Systematic desensitization is a common method used to reduce people's fears and phobias, and it can be used to help you reduce your exam anxiety. It involves first creating a hierarchy (i.e., a list arranged in descending or ascending order) of the various situations that precipitate your exam anxiety and then visualizing these scenarios. Here is how it works:

Constructing Your Anxiety Hierarchy

1. *Buy index cards.* Purchase a stack of index cards, or cut up some cardboard into three-by-four-inch rectangles.

2. *Answer questionnaire.* Use a separate sheet of paper to answer the questionnaire items from the next page.

3. *Cut up your answers.* Cut along each row so that you create strips of paper, each with one item on it.

4. *Ditch some answers.* Throw away the items for which you responded with a "0" as these situations do not cause you anxiety.

5. *Paste answers.* Paste or staple each remaining item on a separate index card or piece of cardboard.

6. *Arrange answers.* Arrange these completed cards ascendingin order from the item that causes you the least anxiety (on the top of the deck) to the one that causes you the most anxiety (on the bottom of the deck).

7. *Number them.* Number the entire deck of cards sequentially, beginning with number 1 on the top of the deck.

Working Through Your Hierarchy

1. *Read.* Read two cards a few times before proceeding to the next step. Which cards you read depends upon where you are in the process of desensitizing yourself to the items in your hierarchy. If you are just beginning, for example, you begin with your cards number 1 and 2. If you already desensitized yourself to cards number 1 and 2, then you would begin with cards number 3 and 4.

2. *Relax.* Close your eyes and get yourself into a relaxed state, using whatever technique feels comfortable for you.

3. *Envision.* Visualize the situation from the first card you read while remaining relaxed. Maintain the visualization for twenty seconds or so. Then stop the visualization and refocus on feelings of relaxation. Repeat the visualization for another twenty seconds and again refocus on feelings of relaxation. If you are able to stay relaxed while visualizing the image from this card twice, you are ready to move onto visualizing your subsequent card. If you're unable to stay relaxed while visualizing this image on these two occasions, return back to the previous card in your hierarchy and work through it again before coming back to the subsequent card.

Note: The entire process of working through the cards successfully may take a number of days or weeks. Following completion, I recommend that you revisit your hierarchy periodically to ensure that you continue to approach exams with less anxiety.

Strategies to Use During the Test

Once you have the exam in front of you, look it over and get a sense of its length and where the marks for the exam are concentrated. It is sometimes helpful to write in time intervals regarding where you ought to be at various points. For example, if the test has fifty multiple choice questions and you have fifty minutes to complete the exam, place a mark at question number 12 (denoting where you should be after approximately twelve minutes, which is quarter time), another mark at question number 25 (half time), and another mark at question number 37 (three quarter time). Also, it is best to answer easier questions first so that you amass confidence, which builds momentum and lowers exam anxiety. Do the hardest questions last.

If you start getting overly anxious during a test, do the following:

1. Use a quick relaxation strategy to calm yourself.

2. Remind yourself that you will do your best, and you can accept this right now.

3. Look for key words in each question and underline or circle them as a way of deepening your focus on the question.

4. If necessary, write on the back of the page anything that may cue your memory.

Creating Your Exam Anxiety Hierarchy

Answer the following questions by circling the number in the column that represents how much anxiety the situation creates for you. Use the following scale:

0 = None, 1 = Mild, 2 = Moderate, 3 = Severe

After completing this, add in any additional situations that cause you exam anxiety.

BEFORE THE TEST

Two days before the exam	0 1 2 3
The night before the exam	0 1 2 3
Going to bed and attempting to sleep the night before the exam	0 1 2 3
Waking up the day of the exam	0 1 2 3
Waiting outside the classroom before the exam	0 1 2 3
Sitting down in my seat before the exam is distributed	0 1 2 3
I find out I need to get an A on the exam in order to pass the course	0 1 2 3

DURING THE TEST

The exam is now in front of me	0 1 2 3
I am looking over the exam	0 1 2 3
I am finding a question difficult to understand	0 1 2 3
I am finding a question difficult to answer	0 1 2 3
I have not been able to answer two questions in a row	0 1 2 3
I am running out of time and I haven't finished the exam	0 1 2 3
There is five minutes left before I have to turn in my exam	0 1 2 3

AFTER THE TEST

I leave the exam believing I have failed it	0 1 2 3
After leaving, I remember the answer to some missed questions	0 1 2 3
The day the exam is returned to me	0 1 2 3

[SPACE FOR ADDITIONAL ITEMS]

	0 1 2 3
	0 1 2 3
	0 1 2 3

▶ Self-Hypnosis Applications

If you start becoming overly anxious during the test, put your pen or pencil down for a minute and use the *REC/TTF* exercise already introduced in Chapter 8. All you do is concentrate on the words, "relaxation, energy, and confidence" (REC) as you breathe in, and on"tension, tiredness, and fear" (TTF) as you breathe out. Anywhere from five to ten breaths is recommended. The more times you have done this before the test, the more you will have conditioned this response—meaning it should become more effective.

Another technique would be to go into self-hypnosis using the basic induction, and then begin giving yourself positive suggestions about having increased confidence, composure, and calmness. You could also create a quick visual image of the way you want to be both feeling and appearing at that moment (i.e., cool, calm, and collected).

Assuming you studied the answer to a question that you find difficult or can't immediately answer, give yourself the following suggestion silently, *"When I return to this question, I will remember the answer to it."* This will act like a post-hypnotic suggestion and will increase the likelihood that the answer will return. (Don't burn this book if it doesn't work every time, however). If you didn't study the answer to a question, give yourself this suggestion instead, *"I don't know the answer to this question, but I do know most of this material."* This suggestion will help keep you from developing brain freeze.

Suggestions/Affirmations

(Note: instructions for using suggestions/affirmations are found in Appendix 6.)

1. I am well prepared for exams and I feel confident in my ability.

2. I feel cool, calm, and collected when I write exams.

3. Preparing and taking exams is often challenging, but I am up for the challenge.

4. I can accept whatever the result is of my performance because I am not perfect.

5. I focus my time and energy on learning and I accept that I do not fully control the outcome. [Note: the reason for this is that you are not the one who constructs the test—a teacher can make a test difficult or easy.]

[Write some of your own below]:

6.

7.

8.

Imagery

(Note: instructions for using imagery are found in Appendix 5.)

When you feel exam anxiety, a very useful visualization is to picture yourself coping well with whatever your "triggers" are. Triggers are the thoughts, images, sensations, situations, or feelings that lead to your exam anxiety. Examples of each of these are: thinking about failing the test (*thought*), daydreaming or dreaming about getting really anxious (*image*), smelling formaldehyde and recalling a failed chemistry exam (*sensation*), being in the actual classroom awaiting to write an exam (*situation*), or feeling depressed about the test and then becoming anxious as you dwell on it (*feeling*).

The images you want to create are the opposite reactions to your triggers. The opposites to the above examples would be:

1. Visualize yourself passing the test (*thought*).

2. Picturing yourself feeling or becoming relaxed and calm (*image*).

3. See yourself smelling formaldehyde and imagine having pleasant thoughts about the next chemistry exam (*sensation*).

4. Envision you are in the classroom while remaining composed, alert, and ready (*situation*).

5. Imagining yourself no longer depressed and feeling capable and calm (*feeling*).

Script

[CAUTION: *If you have a medical condition or physical problem that might prevent you from doing any of the exercises contained in this script, please use a pencil and cross out the part of the script that contains these exercises. If you are uncertain about whether to exclude something, ask your physician* before *making this self-hypnosis tape*]

"Get comfortable, preferably lying down with your arms and legs uncrossed. Now contract all of your muscles simultaneously, and hold the tension [pause for seven breaths]. Now relax your muscles, and notice the contrast between muscle tension and relaxation [pause for four breaths]. Now contract all of your muscles simultaneously again, and hold the tension [pause for seven breaths]. Now relax your muscles, and notice the contrast once more [pause for four breaths].

"With your eyes open, roll your eyes upward slightly (i.e., toward your forehead) so that you feel a mild eye strain, and then stare at a spot while keeping your eyes in that position. Do not let your gaze drift from that spot. Take five deep abdominal breaths [pause for two breaths]. Inhale the fifth breath extra deep, and while holding it, count backwards mentally, '5-4-3-2-1.' When you get down to '1,' exhale and close your eyes at the same time [pause for two breaths].

"You are well prepared for exams and you feel confident in your ability [pause for one breath]. Once you take your seat in the room where you will be writing the exam, you feel a sense of belonging in that seat and this feeling comforts you [pause for one breath]. You become cool, calm, and collected when you write exams [pause for one breath]. The excitement you feel is only about feeling pumped for the challenge you are about to face [pause for two breaths].

"You can accept whatever the result of your performance because you are not perfect [pause for one breath]. Furthermore, you are neither the one who decides what the test will look like nor the one who determines its difficulty level [pause for one breath]. That is why you focus your time and energy on learning and accept that you do not fully control the outcome [pause for one breath]. If you were a surgeon, for example, you would only have control over your knowledge and your performance [pause for one breath]. The outcome is not fully within your control [pause for one breath]. The patient might not improve as a result of the surgery, and something unforeseen could occur [pause for one breath]. Similarly, you only control your learning and your performance, and you can fully accept the outcome, whatever it looks like [pause for two breaths].

"If you need to become more relaxed during an exam, you can simply put your pen or pencil down for a minute, and simultaneously contract all of your muscles [pause for one breath]. Alternatively, you can tilt your eyes back slightly, take five deep abdominal breaths, and then breathe out and close your eyes at the same time [pause for one breath]. Once done, you can tell yourself the messages you need to hear, such as, 'I am regaining my composure and becoming totally focused on this exam. I am here to do my best, and that is what I will do right now' [pause for two breaths].

"If you come to a question that you can't immediately answer, tell yourself, 'When I return to this question, I will remember the answer to it' [pause for one breath]. Then move on to the next question. This will act like a post-hypnotic suggestion and will increase the likelihood that the answer will return [pause for one breath]. If you didn't study the answer to a question, give yourself this suggestion instead, 'I don't know the answer to this question, but I do know most of this material' [pause for 1one-breath]. This suggestion will keep you motivated with momentum [pause for two breaths].

"When you are ready to leave self-hypnosis, first silently tell yourself that you will count to five and that at the count of five, you will come out of self-hypnosis feeling refreshed, relaxed, and confident. Then awaken yourself by counting to five mentally, and say, 'AWAKE!' to yourself [pause for three breaths]. Then open your eyes."

▶ Summary

It is important that you develop a strong sense of your capability to write exams effectively, while at the same time keeping your expectations realistic. A certain amount of anxiety, which can be relabeled as excitement, actually helps you to reach peak efficiency while writing a test. Consequently, the goal of this chapter was not to eliminate exam anxiety, but it to show you how to better manage it and reduce it as needed.

Chapter Ten

Breaking the Block to Better Writing

Arlene has nearly completed all of her coursework for a master's degree in women's studies, but she is struggling to come up with a research topic for her thesis. She begins what soon becomes a frantic search to get focused. After countless hours of reading through journals in her field, she decides on a topic that doesn't really peak her interest. She needs to get her degree done, however, and at least having a topic provides her some momentum.

After three months of doing the necessary research, Arlene is ready to begin writing her thesis. She sits down and begins to stare at the blank computer screen. The sweat forms on her forehead as she strains to find something to write that makes sense to her. Eventually she manages to write two paragraphs, but after reviewing her work a few hours later, she realizes how badly it reads. With a quick touch of the delete key, she is ready to start again. The next few paragraphs she writes seem equally bad, and she again touches the delete key.

A week passes, and Arlene has been unable to write anything of consequence. All that has resulted is that her anxiety level is now at an all time high. Months later,

Arlene has finally completed her thesis, but she is exhausted and is feeling like the entire experience has been a nightmare. After her graduation, she never again opens her thesis. The relief of being done is her only salvation.

You can prevent or escape the incredible frustration Arlene is experiencing. Before you cut off your head, or your fingers, read on. Arlene is having two problems common to students who need to write something: she has difficulty deciding on a topic to write about, and then later experiences "writer's block." Whether you too need to begin a thesis, dissertation, or essay, the issues are the same.

Behind both of these problems is some degree of perfectionism. You want to come up with the perfect topic, and you want your writing to be perfect as well. Perfectionism is never helpful. Remember from Chapter 4 that it is far better to embrace competence than it is to embrace perfectionism, which is beyond the human condition.

Your ability to write becomes increasingly important as you pursue higher levels of education. For writing to become a joy instead of your worst nightmare, three steps are essential. You need to:

- acquire good writing skills,
- explore and decide on good topics,
- develop and sustain writing momentum.

This chapter will explore ways that will help you overcome barriers in these three areas.

▶ Conventional Methods of Overcoming Writer's Block

Acquire Good Writing Skills

Perhaps it is true that some writers are born with the gift of being able to write well. Certainly one's vocabulary, which is highly related to one's overall intellectual ability, is an undeniable factor. More important, however, is knowing that you can also learn to become a good writer. Without question, because of their speed and convenient programs, word processors have revolutionized our ability to improve our writing skills. If you don't own a computer, developing good writing skills will be more difficult for you.

Whether or not you have a computer, two good references to read are:

1. Strunk, W., & White, E. B. (2000). *The Elements of Style* (4th ed.). Toronto: Allyn & Bacon.

2. Waddell, M. L., Esch, R. M., & Walker, R. R. (1993). *The Art of Styling Sentences: 20 Patterns for Success.* Hauppauge, NY: Barrons Educational Series.

The first book is considered a classic and the second is very useful, showing you how to construct more effective, well-balanced sentences. Another great reference to own is as follows:

Merriam-Webster's Collegiate Dictionary (11th ed.). (2003). Springfield, MA: Merriam-Webster.

Since most campuses have adequate computer labs, I am going to assume throughout this chapter that you are using a word processor to do your writing. Three of the most helpful tools in a word processor are the spell check, the grammar check, and the thesaurus. An advantage of the eleventh edition of *Merriam-Webster's Dictionary* is that it contains a CD-ROM that you can load onto your computer. This CD-ROM contains many features not found in a general dictionary, including the ability to search for words that rhyme with a word you are trying to recall. Homophones and synonyms can be searched too, along with several other useful items.

I think the single most important axiom to remember if you want to become a good writer is the title of a book by Joel Salzman called *If You Can Talk, You Can Write.* Throughout this book, Salzman repeatedly makes the point that a great way to start writing is to write something the same way you would say it. The art of writing is really the art of rewriting, so after you get something down the way you would say it, you begin the editing process. Most good writing flows in a way that does sound conversational.

Many times when writing, we become blind to our own glaring mistakes or oversights regarding content or grammar. If you have time, it is always a good idea to put your work away for a few days after completing it before you do another edit on your work. Alternatively, another idea is to ask someone with good writing skills to review your work before you submit it.

Explore and Decide on Good Topics

A *good* topic is one that you feel some for Just as passion is a vital part of becoming successful, it applies to doing good work in other areas. You may want to review Chapter 5 if you still need to foster and get in touch with your passion.

One thing you can do, either alone or with the help of another person, is to brainstorm possible topics. Write these topics down as they are suggested. Another good idea is to carry around a small notepad and pen at all times. When an idea comes to you, write it down. Also keep a notepad and pen by your bedside. Some of the best ideas come to us when we are relaxed and either about to fall asleep or about to wake up. Sometimes great ideas even come to us in our sleep. If an idea does come to you in your sleep, chances are you will wake up because your subconscious knows that you need a topic right now. Write the idea down right away before you forget it.

Another important step in coming up with an exciting topic is to begin doing library and Internet research. Read for a general understanding of the topic that you are considering before doing a detailed reading in the subject area. When you are ready, write out a proposed title for your project and write out the central theme of what it is you want to say in the paper. If you have done enough reading already, you will also be ready to prepare an outline. Once you have an outline, you are ready to begin writing your paper. Here is an example of these three tasks:

Title. How to Cope Better with Stress and Still Have Time for Your Friends

Central Theme. Stress is an unavoidable consequence of living, and how you cope with it makes all the difference. Managing stress allows you to better enjoy your spare time more fully.

Outline.

1. Begin with an anecdote of a time when I was really stressed.

2. Define stress.

3. Look at how stress affects people, both positively and negatively.

4. Review the various stress management strategies:

a) Physical methods—exercise, proper sleep, meditation or relaxation, nutrition;

b) Psychological methods—positive self-talk, talking yourself down, finding humor in the situation or making yourself laugh by going to see a live comedian;

c) Social methods—talking to a friend, seeking social support;

d) Spiritual methods—spending time in prayer, reflecting on what is personally meaningful to you.

5. Look at how better time management can help reduce stress.

6. Argue for the importance of balancing work and play.

7. End with an anecdote of someone with many pressures in her life, but who successfully manages these sources of stress and spends lots of time with her best friends having fun and celebrating life.

Develop and Sustain Writing Momentum

The best way to begin writing is simply to begin writing! Get rid of the notion that your writing will be perfect. By following your outline, you will know how the pieces of your essay will fit together. Many people find that beginning with writing the body of their essay is easier than beginning with the opening paragraph. Find out what works for you.

If you find that you lose writing momentum, you need to ask yourself what is behind the problem. Here are some of the most common reasons with the most common solutions:

Lack of Discipline

Writing requires a high degree of discipline. If you haven't developed discipline yet, read Chapter 6 and follow the instructions there. You will develop discipline as you learn how to persist at your goals; a topic that is addressed in Chapter 6.

Lack of Interest and Boredom

Lack interest and boredom happen far too frequently, particularly when someone else assigns you the topic. Nonetheless, you know the work needs to get done. Read the section in Chapter 6 for overcoming procrastination and use the same techniques listed there. Remember to give yourself rewards for getting chunks of the assignment completed.

Perceived Difficulty

If you believe that the topic you need to write about is going to be too difficult, you will tend to lose your momentum. Again return to Chapter 6 and read the section about procrastination. You need to become more patient with a difficult subject and accept that the writing will take longer.

Exhaustion and Burnout

If you have been burning the proverbial candle at both ends for too long, you suffer the risk of experiencing exhaustion and perhaps even burnout. If this happens, you will need to take a break, and perhaps an extended one. The best plan here is to avoid this depth of fatigue by maintaining a balanced life (see Chapter 7).

Lisa Cohen (n.d.), herself a writer, talked to some prolific writers and extracted the common themes behind the advice they offered to reduce writer's block. The following quote shows what she found:

1. Don't obsess on one thing—have more than one project going at a time and if you get stuck on one, move to another.

2. Commit to finishing everything you start—if you've left a project, commit to returning to it; continue to work on the problem.

3. Change the mode of putting down words—if you're stuck on the word processor try a dictation machine or writing by hand; or change where you write—go outside, or to a friendly coffee shop, or the library.

4. Get some physical exercise—go out and walk; mow the lawn—physical activity of the pleasant and slightly mindless kind seems to precipitate mental activity of the kind that promotes creativity (p. 1).

▶ Self-Hypnosis Applications
Suggestions/Affirmations

(Note: instructions for using suggestions/affirmations are found in Appendix 6.)

Acquiring Good Writing Skills

1. My thinking is becoming clearer, and this results in better writing.

2. I am developing good writing skills.

3. Because I can talk, I can also write.

4. I am motivated to learn more about how to improve my writing.

5. I feel confident in my ability to write, and with proper editing, I too can write well.

[Write some of your own below]:

6.

7.

8.

Exploring and Deciding on Good Topics

1. I am motivated to learn enough about a subject so that I can come up with some good topics.

2. If I haven't chosen a topic yet, my subconscious mind also works hard to give me ideas.

3. If I get to pick my topic, I choose one for which I feel passion.

4. When I am in need of a topic, I carry a notepad with me at all times.

5. Once I have my topic, I write a statement describing the central theme and then I create an outline.

[Write some of your own below]:

6.

7.

8.

Developing and Sustaining Writing Momentum

1. I am developing the necessary discipline to persist in my writing.

2. If the writing project is boring or difficult, I remember to reward myself for getting each step completed.

3. Whenever I am having trouble sustaining my writing, I take a break, get some exercise, or switch to another project for a while.

4. I soon regain the momentum needed to return to writing. The writing project will get done.

5. My writing does not need to be perfect, and neither do I. Instead, I strive to become a competent individual.

[Write some of your own below]:

6.

7.

8.

Imagery

(Note: instructions for using imagery are found in Appendix 5.)

Acquiring Good Writing Skills

Visualize yourself as though you already have good writing skills. Picture the computer screen in front of you, and see yourself typing away with abandon. Imagine the words flowing from your mind onto the screen. Once you have a draft of your project completed, imagine yourself doing a spell check and grammar check on your work.

Exploring and Deciding on Good Topics

First do the necessary reading in the subject area in which you will choose a topic. After you have a fairly good understanding of the area, a very good technique to help you come up with a topic is to place yourself into self-hypnosis using the basic induction (i.e., Appendix 2) and then begin allowing thoughts and images regarding your topic to enter your mind. You might need to prime this activity first by telling yourself, "My entire focus now is on coming up with a good topic for my writing project." The more relaxed you become, the more likely it is you will find this method effective.

Another excellent technique is to give yourself the following suggestion a number of times before going to sleep at night, "My subconscious mind will give me a topic while I am asleep, or first thing upon awakening." This is similar to how many people can awaken themselves at a specific time by programming the time into their mind before they drift off to sleep.

Developing and Sustaining Writing Momentum

Variations of Porter's methods (1978), introduced in Chapter 8, can be useful and used very quickly. If you begin to lose focus while sitting at your computer, pause briefly and say three times firmly and slowly to yourself, "Concentrate and focus." If tension is becoming a problem, use Porter's *relax/let go exercise*. Take five slow deep breaths, thinking at the same time to *relax* as you breathe in and to *let go* as you breathe out.

The other helpful visual image is to picture yourself writing with whatever goal you have in mind. If you want to become a prolific writer, imagine yourself doing lots of writing for extended periods of time. Be sure to create a feeling of enjoyment as you visualize. If your goal is simply to complete a current writing project, visualize writing that project and seeing its completion. It also helps if you picture some of the content of what you intend to write. In this application, it also works as a form of rehearsal for some of the things you want to write.

Much of my writing and the public speaking I have done were imagined before they were ever written or spoken. The inner mind is a wonderful place to rehearse.

Script

[CAUTION: *If you have a medical condition or physical problem that might prevent you from doing any of the exercises contained in this script, please use a pencil and cross out the part of the script that contains these exercises. If you are uncertain about whether to exclude something, ask your physician* before *making this self-hypnosis tape*]

"Get comfortable, preferably lying down with your arms and legs uncrossed. Now contract all of your muscles simultaneously, and hold the tension [pause for seven breaths]. Now relax your muscles, and notice the contrast between muscle tension and relaxation [pause for four breaths]. Now contract all of your muscles simultaneously again, and hold the tension [pause for seven breaths]. Now relax your muscles, and notice the contrast once more [pause for four breaths].

"With your eyes open, roll your eyes upward slightly (i.e., toward your forehead) so that you feel a mild eye strain, and then stare at a spot while keeping your eyes in that position. Do not let your gaze drift from that spot. Take five deep abdominal breaths [pause for two breaths]. Inhale the fifth breath extra deep, and while holding it, count backwards mentally, '5-4-3-2-1.' When you get down to '1,' exhale and close your eyes at the same time [pause for two breaths].

"Your thinking is becoming clearer, and this results in better writing [pause for one breath]. Because you can talk, this means you can write [pause for one breath]. You can now feel confident in your ability to write because with proper editing, you will be writing well [pause for one breath]. You are also motivated to learn more about how to improve your writing [pause for two breaths].

"If you have a writing project to do for which you have no choice on the topic, you develop the necessary discipline to work on it and complete it in a timely manner [pause for one breath].

If necessary, you provide yourself with rewards for getting segments of the project completed [pause for one breath]. If you are given the choice of a topic to write about, you select one for which you feel passion [pause for one breath]. You will find that your subconscious mind helps you in various ways to come up with a good topic [pause for one breath]. It might happen that a great idea is given to you in a dream, or upon awakening [pause for one breath]. It may just be that an idea will pop into your head as you go about your daily routines [pause for one breath]. For these reasons, it is always a good idea to carry around a notepad and a pen with you at all times when you are searching for a topic [pause for two breaths].

"When you need to take a break from writing, you get some exercise or switch to another project for a while [pause for one breath]. Afterwards, you soon regain the momentum needed to return to writing [pause for one breath]. The writing project will get done [pause for one breath]. Your writing doesn't need to be perfect, and neither do you. Instead, you strive to become a competent individual [pause for two breaths].

"When you are ready to leave self-hypnosis, first silently tell yourself that you will count to five and that at the count of five, you will come out of self-hypnosis feeling refreshed, relaxed, and confident. Then awaken yourself by counting to five mentally, and say, 'AWAKE!' to yourself [pause for three breaths]. Then open your eyes."

▶ Summary

Becoming a better writer, choosing worthwhile and meaningful topics to write about, and sustaining the momentum to complete the writing project are important abilities to have as a student, particularly if you plan to pursue postsecondary education. This chapter has shown you a number of ways to develop these skills using conventional methods, followed by ways of using the inner powers of your subconscious mind to help you turn your goals into reality. Write well with less effort than you had imagined.

Chapter Eleven

Finding Your Voice When Giving a Talk

Sarah had been dreading today ever since she knew she would have to give a presentation to her sociology class. The content was not the issue—she had read extensively, written a paper on the topic already, and recited the material out loud several times. It was the thought of having to talk in front of the class that was making her sick to her stomach. It was now her turn to stand and deliver. As she took her place, she felt like she was about to face a firing squad. She could hardly speak. The words were barely forming in her mouth, and worse than that, she began to forget what it was she wanted to say. It took every ounce of courage for Sarah to finish her talk, and she nearly raced back to her seat afterwards. She felt horrible inside and knew she could have done a whole lot better if not for her anxiety.

Speech anxiety is actually the most common fear experienced by the average person. You have probably felt it yourself if you have already delivered one or more presentations. The feeling of being gripped by fear is not uncommon. Candice Thomas (n.d.) reported five common factors that contribute to speech anxiety:

(1) the speaker's previous experience presenting to a group, (2) the fear of being the center of attention, (3) the fear of having others judge your performance, (4) the amount you have prepared for the presentation; and (5) the amount of experience you have presenting to a particular audience or on a specific topic.

A good presentation can be gripping to the audience that hears you, while a poor one can put people to sleep or have them bolting for the door. Regardless of your level of anxiety, there are some things you can do to improve your presentation style and performance, thereby optimizing your grade or at least your impact.

Some nervousness is a good thing: it shows you care about what you are doing and it also creates some excitement within yourself. That excitement, in turn, can be used to garner greater passion in your talk. You don't want to be completely relaxed when you are trying to tell other people something of importance.

▶ Conventional Methods of Reducing Speech Anxiety (and Fostering Better Speaking Skills)

Give a Better Presentation

The Counseling Center for Human Development at the University of South Florida (n.d.) offers the following tips for speakers:

1. *Decide on objectives.* Decide on your specific objectives first.

2. *Use appropriate words.* Put yourself in your audience's place; speak in terms that they'll understand.

3. *Rehearse.* Practice your speech privately. This can help you to feel more confident with what you will say.

4. *Summarize.* Don't memorize or read your speech; use brief notes or an outline.

5. *Make eye contact.* Speak to one person at a time; try to make eye contact with everyone at least once.

6. *Relax.* Don't worry about your hands or your facial expressions.

7. *Talk slowly and easily.* Take it slow and easy, speaking as you do in casual conversation.

8. *Breathe slowly and deeply.* Use slow, deep breathing both before and during your talk to help reduce physical tension.

9. *Seek advice.* Ask for advice and feedback from someone you trust.

Craig (n.d.), an instructor at the University of Iowa, offers additional suggestions:

1. *Practice.* Practice your speech using a detailed outline.

2. *Continue practice.* Continue practicing, using the outline less and increasing eye-contact with your imagined audience.

3. *More practice.* Practice from a key-word outline, reading only direct quotations.

4. *Integrate.* Work on integrating body language and visual aids into your verbal message.

5. *Check timing.* Check the timing of your speech.

6. *Practice with friends.* Practice in front of friends, listen to their advice, and make changes if necessary.

7. *Still more practice.* Practice some more until you feel comfortable and confident.

Other factors to work on include the following (from Craig, n.d.):

1. *Appearance.* You want to dress appropriately for the situation. This will help you feel comfortable in front of your audience.

2. *Facial Expression.* Make sure that your facial expressions serve a purpose.

3. *Voice.* Craig recommends that you work at controling the following vocal properties:

a) *Volume.* Speak at an appropriate volume, and vary it for emphasis.

b) *Pitch.* This refers to how high or low your voice is (e.g., bass versus treble). Effective speakers strive to use their *optimal pitch* as the base for their speech, although they vary it as well for emphasis. Optimal pitch is four or five notes above the lowest note you can sing.

c) *Rhythm.* Rhythm is determined by your use of volume and

pitch. Avoid using a "singsong" pattern, but give your rhythm some variation as well. A monotone voice is not desirable either.

d) *Tempo.* This is the rate at which you make sounds. People in the southern states, for example, generally speak slower than those in the northern states. Learn to vary your tempo and use pauses for emphasis.

e) *Articulation and enunciation.* You want everyone to understand you, so you work at correctly pronouncing words as well.

Reduce Speech Anxiety

The same methods used to reduce exam anxiety are used for reducing speech anxiety:

1. Relaxation Techniques,
2. Cognitive Therapy,
3. Systematic Desensitization Therapy,
4. Imagery (as imagery is a self-hypnotic technique, it will be covered in the next section).

Relaxation Techniques
You will find relaxation methods in Appendices 2, 5, and 7.

Cognitive Therapy
We reviewed the triple-column technique in Chapter 4, and the following instructions show how to apply it to speech anxiety:

MALADAPTIVE THOUGHT OR BELIEF	QUESTIONING IT	HEALTHY THOUGHT OR BELIEF
"I can't stand to talk in front of my class. They will see how nervous I am."	"What evidence do I have that indicates I cannot give a presentation? I may not enjoy the experience, but I will get through it. Even though I will be nervous, it will be more obvious to me than to them. Who cares anyways? Most of them are also nervous when speaking.	"I am capable of giving an effective speech. Even if I am nervous, I can still deliver a good talk."

This is how you use the triple-column:

1. Write out the thought(s) or belief(s) that is causing you to feel anxious in the first column. You might already be aware of some of these thoughts, in which case you can record them now. Another approach is to wait until something triggers you to feel anxious before making an entry.

2. In the second column, challenge the logic behind your thought or belief. Use the questions below to help you do this:

a) What proof do I have that this thought is true?

b) Do I have any evidence that indicates it is not true?

c) Are there any competing "truths?" Is another belief just as valid?

d) Does everyone think this way? Why, or why not?

e) Does agreeing with the majority in this belief make it necessarily correct?

f) Where did I learn this message? Is it possible that the messenger was wrong?

g) What purpose is served in continuing to believe this?

h) What price do I pay for continuing to believe this?

i) What are the advantages of believing something different?

j) Are my feelings about this issue providing an accurate gauge of what I should believe?

k) If I was helping someone else deal with this, what would I want him to believe?

l) If I knew I would be dead tomorrow, would I be happy believing this?

Once you have challenged your thinking, write out the challenge in the second column.

3. In the third column, write out a healthy thought(s) or belief(s) that you would like to substitute for the one written in the first column.

4. Spend time focusing on the thought(s) or belief(s) written in the third column. The more you absorb yourself in repeating the thought(s) or belief(s), the more you will internalize it.

5. Whenever you catch yourself repeating similar anxious thoughts to yourself, either write them down again and repeat steps 2 through 5, or do the work in your head by talking to yourself, either silently or out loud. Remember to do both the challenge and then to substitute the healthy thought or belief.

Systematic Desensitization Therapy

Repeated here (from Chapter 9) are the instructions for how this method works:

Constructing Your Anxiety Hierarchy

1. Purchase a stack of index cards, or cut up some cardboard into three-by-four-inch rectangles.

2. Use a separate sheet of paper to answer the questionnaire items from the next page.

3. Cut along each row so that you create strips of paper, each with one item on it.

4. Throw away the items for which you responded with a "0" as these situations do not cause you anxiety.

5. Paste or staple each remaining item on a separate index card or piece of cardboard.

6. Arrange these completed cards in order from the item that causes you the least anxiety on the top of the deck to the one that causes you the most anxiety on the bottom of the deck.

7. Number the entire deck of cards sequentially, beginning with number 1 on the top of the deck.

Working Through Your Hierarchy

1. *Read.* Read two cards a few times before proceeding to the next step. Which cards you read depends upon where you are in desensitizing yourself to the items in your hierarchy. If you are just beginning, for example, you begin with your cards number 1 and 2. If you already desensitized yourself to cards number 1 and 2, then you would begin with cards number 3 and 4.

2. *Relax.* Close your eyes and get yourself into a relaxed state, using whatever technique feels comfortable for you.

3. *Envision.* Visualize the situation from the first card you read while you remain relaxed. Maintain the visualization for twenty seconds or so. Then stop the visualization and refocus on feelings of relaxation. Repeat the visualization for another twenty seconds and again refocus on feelings of relaxation. If you are able to stay relaxed while visualizing the image from this card twice, you are ready to move onto visualizing your subsequent card. If you're unable to stay relaxed while visualizing this image on these two occasions, return back to the previous card in your hierarchy and work through it again before coming back to the subsequent card.

Note: The entire process of working through the cards successfully may take a number of days or weeks. Following completion, I recommend that you revisit your hierarchy periodically to ensure that you continue to approach presentations with less anxiety.

CREATING YOUR SPEECH ANXIETY HIERARCHY

Answer the following questions by circling the number in the column that represents how much anxiety the situation creates for you. Use the following scale:

0 = None, 1 = Mild, 2 = Moderate, 3 = Severe

After completing this, add in any additional situations that cause you speech anxiety.

BEFORE THE SPEECH

Two days before the speech	0 1 2 3
The night before the speech	0 1 2 3
Going to bed and attempting to sleep the night before the speech	0 1 2 3
Waking up the day of the speech	0 1 2 3
Waiting outside the classroom before the speech	0 1 2 3
Walking to the front of the class to deliver my speech	0 1 2 3
I find out I need to get an A on the speech in order to pass the course	0 1 2 3

DURING THE SPEECH

I am now standing in front of the class and about to begin talking	0 1 2 3

I am looking at everyone in the classroom before I begin speaking	0 1 2 3
I am beginning to say the first words of my speech	0 1 2 3
I have lost the notes for my speech and will need to ad lib	0 1 2 3
I am about to speak in front of 200 students	0 1 2 3
I can tell that my speech is not being received well by the audience	0 1 2 3
A local television station has asked you to speak on camera	0 1 2 3

AFTER THE SPEECH

I leave the speech believing I have done a poor job	0 1 2 3
After leaving, I remember some important points I forgot to include	0 1 2 3
My grade for the speech is less than I expected	0 1 2 3

[SPACE FOR ADDITIONAL ITEMS]

	0 1 2 3
	0 1 2 3
	0 1 2 3

▶ Self-Hypnosis Applications

If you start becoming overly anxious during the speech, use the REC/TTF exercise already introduced in Chapter 8. All you would do is concentrate on the words, "relaxation, energy, and confidence" (REC) as you breathe in, and "tension, tiredness, and fear" (TTF) as you breathe out. Anywhere from five to ten breaths are recommended. The more times you have done this before the speech, the more you will have conditioned this response—meaning it should become more effective.

Suggestions/Affirmations

(Note: instructions for using suggestions/affirmations are found in Appendix 6.)

1. I am motivated to prepare adequately before giving a speech.

2. I feel cool, calm, and collected when I talk before an audience.

3. I am okay with being the center of attention periodically.

4. I feel passionate about the speech that I will deliver.

5. My speech doesn't have to be perfect—I will do the best that I can, and that will suffice.

[Write some of your own below]:

6.

7.

8.

Imagery

(Note: instructions for using imagery are found in Appendix 5.)

The more you visualize yourself giving an effective speech or presentation, the more your anxiety will diminish. The important thing to remember is to give it as much detail as you can. Imagine having confidence in both how you feel and in how you posture yourself. Picture the passion you feel and see it come across as you get into your talk. See the audience responding to you, and see yourself responding to the audience. Picture familiar faces hearing and watching your speech. Notice them paying attention to you. See them, smiling with interest. Overall, get in touch with the awareness that your audience is supportive of you.

Imagery is also an excellent forum for practicing all aspects of your speech: use it to rehearse the things you want to say, and the way you want to say them. Imagine all the aspects of giving a good speech that were introduced earlier in the conventional methods section (e.g., appearance, voice dynamics).

Script

[CAUTION: *If you have a medical condition or physical problem that might prevent you from doing any of the exercises contained in this script, please use a pencil and cross out the part of the script that contains these exercises. If you are uncertain about whether to exclude something, ask your physician before making this self-hypnosis tape*]

"Get comfortable, preferably lying down with your arms and legs uncrossed. Now contract all of your muscles simultaneously, and hold the tension [pause for seven breaths]. Now relax your muscles, and notice the contrast between muscle tension and relaxation [pause for four breaths]. Now contract all of your muscles simultaneously again, and hold the tension [pause for seven breaths]. Now relax your muscles, and notice the contrast once more [pause for four breaths].

"With your eyes open, roll your eyes upward slightly (i.e., toward your forehead) so that you feel a mild strain, and then stare at a spot while keeping your eyes in that position. Do not let your gaze drift from that spot. Take five deep abdominal breaths [pause for two breaths]. Inhale the fifth breath extra deep, and while holding it, count backwards mentally, '5-4-3-2-1.' When you get down to '1,' exhale and close your eyes at the same time [pause for two breaths].

"Whenever you are to give a speech or presentation, you prepare extensively for it [pause for one breath]. You learn your material well so that the content is mostly committed to memory [pause for one breath]. You also practice your speech several times, both out loud and in your imagination [pause for one breath]. You remember to use relaxation exercises, such as abdominal breathing, to help you become comfortable before getting up to give your presentation [pause for two breaths].

"Rather than having your speech written out word-for-word,

you instead have a key-word outline in front of you [pause for one breath]. You are amazed that although you feel some excitement before giving your talk, you soon become cool, calm, and collected in front of your audience [pause for one breath]. Your passion also comes through, however, as you find ways to modulate your voice dynamics to enhance interest [pause for two breaths].

"You are finding that it is okay to become the center of attention when you give a talk [pause for one breath]. Although people's eyes are focused on you, they are mostly focused on what you have to say [pause for one breath]. You speak with confidence and authority—you find your voice, and your voice is strong and impactful [pause for one breath]. You have something to say, and you want to say it when given the opportunity [pause for one breath]. With practice, you find that you begin enjoying giving speeches and presentations [pause for two breaths].

"When you are ready to leave self-hypnosis, first silently tell yourself that you will count to five and that at the count of five, you will come out of self-hypnosis feeling refreshed, relaxed, and confident. Then awaken yourself by counting to five mentally, and say 'AWAKE!' to yourself [pause for three breaths]. Then open your eyes."

▶ Summary

Public speaking anxiety is the most common fear experienced by the average person. This chapter has shown you methods to help you give a better presentation, and it has also shown you both conventional and hypnotic methods for reducing speech anxiety. By following the suggestions outlined here, you will begin to find your voice when giving a talk.

Chapter Twelve

Sleeping Through Your Career Search

Jared was told all his life that he would follow in his father's footsteps by becoming a physician. An admirable profession, Jared thought, but not one that he was particularly interested in. His interests really seemed to find expression in the arts, especially drama. Jared took drama throughout junior and senior high school, and drama teachers occasionally told him that he had real talent. He thought that acting would become his career, but his dad nearly had a coronary when he was told the news. In no uncertain terms Dad said that acting was an unacceptable career choice, and Jared would instead enroll in pre-medical education. Despite his own wishes, Jared could understand the logic of what his father was insisting upon.

Jared began pre-med, and although he hated chemistry, biology, and math, he was gifted and this meant he could succeed at nearly any career choice. His grades and letters of recommendation eventually did lead him into the faculty of medicine, and a few years later he graduated and became a family practitioner. Jared enjoyed his income immensely. When he wasn't working, however, he often felt that his energy and joy were. The thought of having to return to work was almost sickening, but how could he change careers now that he had invested so many years into becoming a doctor? He began looking for ways to help himself cope better, and drugs were easy enough to come by. The drugs seemed to help, but what really helped him feel better was drinking an entire bottle of vodka every night.

Twenty years later, Jared began feeling a pain in his lower back. He ignored it as long as he could, but was soon forced to seek medical help. He had incurable liver disease, and within six months was dead. Everyone who attended the funeral said he seemed like such an unhappy soul, despite his prestigious and successful career. No one could understand it.

There are some decisions in life that have a profound impact on our health and our happiness. One of these decisions is the lifestyle decision we make, another is our choice of an intimate other, and still another is our career choice. As most of us spend the best part of our waking hours working in our careers—and our careers provide the financial resources necessary to have an optimal lifestyle that may also help us attract a worthy mate— perhaps our career choice determines our happiness more than any other life decision.

Using a very large sample of individuals, Holland and Gottfredson (cited in Morgan & Skovholt, 1977) found that a person's top occupational daydream is often more predictive of his or her eventual career choice than scores on the *Self-Directed Search*, a popular career interest test. Wilson and Eddy (1982) claimed that knowing oneself may be more important in decision making than knowing the world of work. Most career practitioners would agree that both factors are of significant importance, and this chapter will look at how you can enhance your ability to make a good career decision.

Making an appropriate career choice is important for academic success. Once you know which career you feel passionate about, you will begin feeling motivated to excel in school. Without a goal that extends beyond your education, it is difficult to work hard because school can seem removed from real life at times. If you are going to work hard at something, it may as well be something that takes you to your own destination.

▶ Conventional Methods of Fostering Career Choice

In addition to whatever steps you take on your own, making an appointment with your guidance counselor is highly recommended when you are ready to make a career decision. Looking at the career exploration process in depth is beyond the scope of this section of the book, but it generally follows four steps. The Internet websites included in the following four steps do contain in-depth information, however, if you are interested in reading more on the subject:

1. *Increase self-awareness.* The more you know about yourself, the easier it will become to make a good career decision. A guidance counselor at your school may have a number of tests, inventories, and questionnaires for you to complete that will help you become more aware of your interests, personality, aptitudes, values, and other important factors to consider in making your choice. Some good Internet sites to help you increase your self-awareness are as follows:

a) Career Planning Guides

- http://10steps.careerpathsonline.com/index.asp (Note: you will need to create a log-in profile)
- http://www.princetonreview.com/cte/quiz/career_quiz1.asp
- http://www.adm.uwaterloo.ca
- http://admn.santafe.cc.fl.us/~crc/webasses.htm

b) Personality Preference Guides

- http://typefocus.com
- http://www.humanmetrics.com/cgi-win/JTypes1.htm
- http://www.keirsey.com
- www.personalitypage.com

2. *Learn about the world of work.* The more you know about the career opportunities available, the better chance you will have of making a good career decision. Some good Internet sites to help you explore career possibilities are as follows:

a) In Canada
- www.workinfonet.ca
- http://www.hrdc-drhc.gc.ca
- http://www23.hrdc-drhc.gc.ca/2001/e/generic/welcome.shtml

b) In the United States
- http://www.dictionary-occupationaltitles.net
- http://online.onetcenter.org

3. *Come up with a list of possible career choices.* For this process it helps to both use lists of career titles and to brainstorm either alone or preferably with others who know you well.

4. *Evaluate the choices and making a career decision.* This is probably the hardest step in career exploration because it means weighing everything you know about yourself against what each career choice you are considering has to offer.

▶ Self-Hypnosis Applications

Several writers have commented on the usefulness of using imagery work within the realm of career counseling (Morgan & Skovholt, 1977; Owen & Wilson, 1980; Reupert & Maybery, 2000; Sarnoff & Remer, 1982; Wilson & Eddy, 1982). One of the common themes expressed in these articles is that imagery helps people improve their self-awareness. Sarnoff and Remer (1982) used guided imagery to help clients generate career alternatives, and they found that this group produced more alternatives compared to a discussion control group. They concluded that guided imagery promotes divergent thinking.

Suggestions/Affirmations

(Note: instructions for using suggestions/affirmations are found in Appendix 6.)

1. I am motivated to take the necessary steps to learn more about myself and my interests.

2. I am motivated to take the necessary steps to learn more about the world of work and about career opportunities.

3. My mind often takes me to thinking about my career options.

4. There is no one perfect career choice, but there are several good choices for me that I need to discover.

5. My dreams sometimes reveal interesting career choices to me, and I remember them in the morning so that I can write them down.

[Write some of your own below]:

6.

7.

8.

Imagery

(Note: instructions for using imagery are found in Appendix 5.)

I have organized this section according to the use of imagery work during three periods of career development: before a career decision is made (i.e., *Pre-Career Choice*), during the decision-making process (i.e., *Career Choice*), and during the time you are beginning your job search (i.e., *Job Searching*).

Pre-Career Choice

1. *Increase self-confidence.* Imagery suggested while in the hypnotic state has been used successfully to increase a woman's self-confidence to later make a career decision (Reupert & Maybery, 2000). As you probably suspect by now, self-hypnosis is equally effective for men, so consequently, applications of self-hypnosis-to career choice will work equally well for either gender (i.e. it should work even if you don't know your gender)! Improving self-confidence is a common goal of hypnotic intervention (Hartland, 1971).

2. *Improve self-esteem.* An entire book has been written about

how imaging and self-hypnosis can be used to improve a person's self-esteem (Napier, 1990). Hartland (1971) also writes about this phenomenon.

3. *Enhance self-awareness.* Enhancing self-awareness was mentioned earlier as a frequently referred-to application of imaging within career counseling work.

Career Choice

1. *Increase creativity.* As mentioned earlier, Sarnoff and Remer (1982) found that guided imagery was more helpful in generating career alternatives compared to a discussion control group. Other research conducted by Raikov (1976) suggested that creativity in subjects can be enhanced in those capable of deep hypnosis.

2. *Enhance career exploration.* Imagery, whether guided or self-directed, is a wonderful way of having clients visualize themselves performing different careers. You can imagine yourself going through a typical day that someone in a specific career would experience. It may be the next best thing to job shadowing. Wilson and Eddy (1982) had clients imagine themselves in a particular job, and then asked them questions like, *"Picture in your mind how your life would be: What sort of things are you doing? What would you be doing differently than now? Where are you living? How is your life style different? How do other people act toward you?"* (p. 293).

3. *Put ideas into the unconscious for answers.* Our unconscious minds often provide us the answers we are looking for—all we need to do is ask. One way of using this technique is to ask yourself for career possibilities whenyou retire to bed. You may find that something that comes to you in a dream is helpful, or you may wake up with a few career-related thoughts already in your mind.

Job Searching

1. *Prepare for job interviews.* I have used this technique myself. While you are in a relaxed state, imagine yourself in the job inter-

view situation, visualizing as fully as possible how composed and confident you will feel. You then anticipate the questions that may be asked of you, and how you will respond to these, imagining both the verbal (what you will say) and the nonverbal aspects (voice dynamics, facial expression, etc.).

2. *Make a choice between different job offers.* Similar to the idea presented in *enhancing career exploration* described earlier, here you visualize doing each job on a typical day. You can also put the choice to your unconscious for answers, and then sleep on it.

Some Useful Visualizations

Below are some visual images that have been used by various researchers and practitioners for career counseling:

1. *Images of a place.* Using this technique, you imagine "a beautiful outdoor place, flying to any part of the world, and visiting the future" (Skovholt, Morgan, & Negron-Cunningham, 1989, p. 303).

2. *Images of yourself at the end of your career.* Write a soliloquy about what you have accomplished in your life; how you have felt about these accomplishments, your secret hopes, feelings, and dreams; and how you and the world have changed (Torrance & Reynolds, p. 42, cited in Gerler, 1980).

3. *The "Day in the Future" Fantasy* (Morgan & Skovholt, 1977). This visualization is guided imagery that asks you to imagine all of the events that occur to you, from morning till night, during a typical work day five, ten, or fifteen years from now.

4. *The "Award Ceremony" Fantasy* (Morgan & Skovholt). You imagine you are receiving a special award for a special competence. The fantasy is said to help you get in touch with your goals and motivation.

5. *The "Opposite Sex" Fantasy* (Morgan & Skovholt). You imagine you are the opposite sex performing work-related activities. The fantasy is meant to diminish gender stereotypes in choosing a career.

6. *Time projection.* Reupert and Maybery (2000) used three

techniques with a woman who was seen for career counseling, using hypnosis as the medium. Borrowing from other writers, they used time projection (similar to the "Day in the Future" Fantasy), going to a special place (and receiving a "special gift" from the unconscious), and listening to an older and wiser version of herself (reported as a common technique with therapists).

7. *Images of your own death.* This technique uses an image I suggested earlier in Chapter 5 focused on getting in touch with the purpose or meaning of your life. This can be done in numerous ways, one of which is to imagine what you want said in your eulogy after your death. What do you want to be remembered for?

Script

[CAUTION: *If you have a medical condition or physical problem that might prevent you from doing any of the exercises contained in this script, please use a pencil and cross out the part of the script that contains these exercises. If you are uncertain about whether to exclude something, ask your physician* before *making this self-hypnosis tape*]

"Get comfortable, preferably lying down with your arms and legs uncrossed. Now contract all of your muscles simultaneously, and hold the tension [pause for seven breaths]. Now relax your muscles, and notice the contrast between muscle tension and relaxation [pause for four breaths]. Now contract all of your muscles simultaneously again, and hold the tension [pause for seven breaths]. Now relax your muscles, and notice the contrast once more [pause for four breaths].

"With your eyes open, roll your eyes upward slightly (i.e., toward your forehead) so that you feel a mild eye strain, and then stare at a spot while keeping your eyes in that position. Do not let your gaze drift from that spot. Take five deep abdominal breaths [pause for two breaths]. Inhale the fifth breath extra deep, and while holding it, count backwards mentally, '5-4-3-2-1.' When you get down to '1,' exhale and close your eyes at the same time [pause for two breaths].

"Finding a suitable career choice is one of the most important decisions you will make in your life [pause for one breath]. You recognize that there is no one perfect career choice, but there are several good choices that you need to discover [pause for one breath]. It is imperative that you spend sufficient time on this task so that you come up with an appropriate career plan [pause for one breath]. Consequently, you are motivated to take the necessary steps to learn more about yourself and your interests [pause for one breath]. You also feel motivated to take the necessary steps to learn more about the world of work and about career opportunities [pause for two breaths].

"Often your mind takes you to thinking about your career options [pause for one breath]. Sometimes you find yourself fantasizing about working in different careers [pause for one breath]. Your dreams sometimes reveal interesting career choices to you, and you remember them in the morning so that you can write them down [pause for one breath]. Both your conscious and subconscious minds are working together as a team to help you with this goal [pause for two breaths].

"Not only do you use imagery to help you to consider different career alternatives, but you also use it to prepare for job interviews [pause for one breath]. You envisage yourself in the job interview situation itself, visualizing as fully as possible how composed and confident you feel [pause for one breath]. You also anticipate questions that might be asked of you, and how you will respond to these questions [pause for one breath]. You include the nonverbal aspects as well, such as having a steady calm voice, and having appropriate voice volume, voice tone, facial expressions, and body posture [pause for two breaths].

"When you are ready to leave self-hypnosis, first silently tell yourself that you will count to five and that at the count of five, you will come out of self-hypnosis feeling refreshed, relaxed, and confident. Then awaken yourself by counting to five mentally, and say 'AWAKE!' to yourself [pause for three breaths]. Then open your eyes."

▶ **Summary**

Besides the many conscious processes you use to help you in deciding upon a suitable career choice, you can also rely on self-hypnosis for helping to get properly motivated to begin thinking about careers, for assistance in coming up with viable career options, and for preparing for job interviews. If knowledge of self is indeed more important in career decision-making than knowledge of the world of work, the use of imagery has the added advantage in the many ways it can enhance self-awareness. I encourage you to try it.

Epilogue

More Power to You

Einstein said, "When I examine myself and my methods of thought, I come to the conclusion that the gift of fantasy has meant more to me than my talent for absorbing positive knowledge."
(Dreistadt, as cited in Bowers & Bowers, 1979, p. 359).

You are now at the end of your next beginning. Succeeding in school and in life doesn't have to be as difficult as you may have thought when you began this book. It remains challenging, but challenging is not the same as grueling. After you master the success formula, you will feel the inner power that is released from succeeding at one goal after another. Each success strengthens your resolve to enjoy yet another success and still another. coupled with the mental and emotional gains are the increases in stamina that you will experience.

This book has shown you how to improve several major areas that ultimately lead to higher grades. Through both tried and true conventional methods and through the best of what we know about self-hypnosis, this book has armed you with a plethora of techniques to help you succeed at your goals.

As this is the first edition, your feedback is important to me. If there is something you found particularly helpful, or not helpful, let me know—I would love to hear from you. You can contact me by sending an e-mail to alderson@ucalgary.ca. Your feedback will be incorporated into the next edition of *Grade Power*.

Perhaps you will never sing like the friend about whom I wrote about in the preface. Perhaps you will never dance either. But know that if there was something you ever really wanted to do, you could do it, and that self-hypnosis could be your ally in your quest to become more of who you want to become. Success is about believing in yourself, feeling passion for your goals, persisting in attaining them, and keeping a balanced lifestyle most of the time. Now is your time—make it the best it could ever be: you deserve it.

Appendix One

How to Make and Use Your Own Recorded Scripts

In addition to the major scripts that follow these instructions, there are shorter scripts suggested throughout this book. The instructions for recording and using those scripts are the same as for the Major Scripts.

▶ Making Scripts
Voice Dynamics

Remember—you will be recording scripts that are intended to serve a purpose, the first of which is to help you relax. Your voice dynamics will have some effect on the result. Before you begin recording, practice getting your voice into the following state:

1. *Relaxed and slow.* You will want to talk slowly on the tape and sound as if you are already relaxed. Get relaxed before you start taping.

2. *Monotone.* The more monotone the sound of your voice, the better. Practice talking at the same pitch, with little variety in your tone. It can be effective to lower your pitch toward the end of each sentence if you prefer, but it is unnecessary.

3. *Deeper tone.* Another helpful, but unnecessary, voice dynamic is

a deeper tone of voice. Practice talking in a somewhat deeper voice than you normally use.

Pause Conventions

To make an effective tape, you will want to allow pauses of various lengths between the sentences that you read during the recording. The script tells you whether to pause for one, two, or three breaths after each sentence. To pause for one breath, simply wait until you have exhaled the next breath before continuing with your reading of the next sentence. To pause for two or three breaths, wait for two or three exhaled breaths before continuing. The instructions are given in square brackets; they are actions to be completed—*not* commands to be read aloud.

Recording

When you are ready, proceed with the following steps:

Step 1. *Set Up Equipment and Make Sure It Works*—be sure everything is working before you begin. Test the equipment out by recording a few lines and then playing it back.

Step 2. *Begin Reading the Script*—use the voice dynamics you practiced earlier. Remember to pause for the appropriate length according to the conventions described above.

▶ Using Scripts

Hypnosis and self-hypnosis create change when deeply held attitudes, beliefs, and behavior change. This takes time, and that is why *repetition* of suggestions and imagery is important. Listen to your recordings whenever you have time to relax safely. It is *not* safe to listen to the tapes while you are driving, for example. The deeper you become conditioned for self-hypnosis, the greater will be the depth of relaxation you feel while listening to your recordings. Be sure you are in comfortable surroundings where you don't have to do anything other than relax.

It is generally best to listen to a recording on a daily basis to enhance the repetition of the suggestions and imagery. You will know if it is helping you after you have been consistent in listening to it for at least a week. If it is not helping you, you may want to spend more time on the other techniques described in this book for dealing with the particular area you are wanting to improve.

Appendix Two

The Basic Induction for Self-Hypnosis

▸ Preliminary Practice

Spend some time practicing the following three components of self-hypnosis separately before moving to the basic induction itself. These three components are:

- simultaneous muscle contraction
- deep abdominal breathing
- relaxing visual imagery

1. *Simultaneous muscle contraction.* Contract as many muscles as you can at the same time. This should involve doing the following actions simultaneously:

- scrunching your face together,
- pulling your shoulders up as high as possible,
- tightening your hands into fists and straightening your arms,
- flattening your abdomen and making it rigid,
- tightening the muscles in your buttocks,
- straightening your legs and pressing your heels down.

Hold the muscle tension for twenty seconds, then relax your muscles for ten seconds, paying attention to the contrast in how your now muscles feel. Repeat by tensing your muscles again for twenty seconds followed by ten seconds of noting the contrast in how your muscles now feel.

2. *Deep abdominal breathing.* Do the following activities, one step at a time:

a) Regulate your normal breathing cycle by making it slow, steady, and rhythmical. When you are anxious, your breathing will become choppy. The kind of breathing you want to create is where air enters your lungs at the same pace and is exhaled from your lungs similarly.

b) Begin deep breathing. There is no need to hold any of these breaths.

c) Place one hand on your stomach.

d) Now when you inhale, make your stomach rise as much as you can. This is done by letting your stomach puff out as you breathe inward. It will feel as though you are breathing air into your stomach. Mostly what is happening is that you are breathing air into both the top and bottom portions of your lungs. We call this abdominal breathing, and it is the most relaxing form of breathing due to the greater amount of oxygen inhaled.

3. *Relaxing visual imagery.* Spend some time relaxing while you create relaxing visual images in your mind. This is the same thing as daydreaming, except you fully direct the visualizations. Here are some samples of relaxing images you could use:

- lying on a beach,
- hiking through a forest,
- scuba diving,
- feeding birds,
- walking barefoot in a park,
- relaxing in a Jacuzzi.

Imagery is best accomplished by introducing as many senses and details into your visualizations as possible. For example, if you imagine yourself lying on a beach, see the blue sky and blue water (i.e., sights), hear the rhythmical sound of ocean waves crashing into shore (i.e., sounds), remember the feeling of warm sand under your hands and feet (i.e., touch), smell the fresh ocean air (i.e., smell), and recreate the sense of tranquility (i.e., feelings). The more vivid your visualization, the more deeply you'll relax.

▶ The Basic Induction Method

After you've practiced the previously noted three components of self-hypnosis a number of times over a number of occasions, and you feel that you have done each one satisfactorily, then it is time to integrate these pieces. There are many different ways to go into self-hypnosis. The advantage of the basic induction method presented here is that it will help you relax your body and mind quickly, and thereby enter self-hypnosis quickly as well. Once you become proficient in attaining a deep state of relaxation following this method, you may wish to shorten the induction further. A simpler induction might include only steps three and four, for example. Let depth be your gauge in deciding whether to shorten the induction eventually.

Follow these instructions:

1. *Get comfortable.* Get comfortable, preferably lying down with your arms and legs uncrossed.

2. *Contract your muscles simultaneously.* Hold the muscle tension for twenty seconds; then relax your muscles for ten seconds, paying attention to the contrast in how your muscles feel. Repeat by tensing again for twenty seconds, followed by ten seconds of noticing the contrast between muscle tension and relaxation.

3. *Fixate your eyes.* With your eyes open, roll your eyes upward slightly (i.e., toward your forehead) so that you feel a mild eye strain, and then stare at a spot while keeping your eyes in that position. Do not let your gaze drift from that spot.

4. *Engage in deep abdominal breathing before eye closure.* Take in five deep abdominal breaths. Inhale the fifth breath extra deep, and while holding it, count backwards mentally, "5-4-3-2-1." When you get down to "1," exhale and close your eyes at the same time.

5. *Create a relaxing visual image.* Spend at least five minutes focusing on a relaxing visual image.

6. *Exit the self-hypnotic state.* When you are ready to leave self-hypnosis, first silently tell yourself that you will count to five and that at the count of five, you will come out of self-hypnosis feel-

ing refreshed, relaxed, and confident. Then awaken yourself by counting to five mentally, and say, "AWAKE!" to yourself. Then open your eyes.

That's it! What you do with this state is explained throughout this book.

Appendix Three

Major Script #1: "The Basics of Self-Hypnosis"

Record this script using the instructions in Appendix 2 (found on the preceding page). If you have a medical condition or physical problem that might prevent you from doing any of the exercises contained in this script, please use a pencil and cross out the part of the script that contains these exercises. If you are uncertain about whether to exclude something, ask your physician before making this self-hypnosis tape. Alternatively, feel free to alter the script in a way that makes the experience safe and pleasurable for you. As soon as you're ready, begin.

Record the following script:

"Either sit down or lie down on a comfortable surface. Uncross your arms and legs. Your eyes may be either open or closed [pause for one breath]. Let yourself relax, and know that for right now, there is nothing more important than letting go [pause for one breath]. Let go of all thoughts, all worries, all stress [pause for one breath]. This is your time to relax [pause for one breath].

"In a few moments, I will ask you to contract as many muscles as you can at the same time [pause for one breath]. This involves

doing the following actions simultaneously:
- scrunching your face together,
- pulling your shoulders up as high as possible,
- tightening your hands into fists and straightening your arms,
- flattening your abdomen and making it rigid,
- tightening the muscles in your buttocks,
- straightening your legs and pressing your heels down [pause for one breath].

"Okay, let's begin. Scrunch your face, pull your shoulders up, tighten your hands into fists and straighten your arms, flatten your stomach and make it hard, tighten the muscles in your buttocks, and straighten your legs and press your heels down [pause for one breath]. Hold the tension [pause for two breaths]. Hold the tension [pause for two breaths]. A few more seconds [pause for two breaths]. Keep holding [pause for two breaths].

"And now release the tension, let your muscles relax, and concentrate on the difference, on how relaxed your muscles feel by contrast [pause for one breath]. Notice how your body feels—relaxed, calm, perhaps tired, perhaps fatigued [pause for one breath]. All parts of your body are now relaxed [pause for one breath]. Face relaxed, shoulders and arms relaxed, stomach relaxed, legs and buttocks relaxed [pause for one breath].

"Now let's repeat the muscle contractions [pause for one breath]. Scrunch your face, pull your shoulders up, tighten your hands into fists and straighten your arms, flatten your stomach and make it hard, tighten the muscles in your buttocks, and straighten your legs and press your heels down [pause for one breath]. Hold the tension [pause for two breaths]. Hold the tension [pause for two breaths]. A few more seconds [pause for two breaths]. Keep holding [pause for two breaths].

"And now release the tension, let your muscles relax, and concentrate on the difference, on how relaxed your muscles feel by contrast [pause for one breath]. Notice how your body feels—relaxed, calm, perhaps tired, perhaps fatigued [pause for one breath]. All parts of your body are now relaxed [pause for one breath]. Face relaxed, shoulders and arms relaxed, stomach relaxed, legs and buttocks relaxed [pause for one breath]. Your whole body is relaxed now [pause for one breath].

"In a few moments, I will ask you to take five deep abdominal breaths [pause for one breath]. Before you begin this, I want you to regulate your normal breathing cycle by making it slow, steady, and rhythmical [pause for three breaths]. You want air to enter your lungs at a slow steady pace, and you want it to exit your lungs at a slow steady pace [pause for one breath]. Inhale deeply and slowly, and exhale deeply and slowly [pause for two breaths]. Inhale deeply and slowly, exhale deeply and slowly [pause for two breaths].

"Now, with your eyes open, roll your eyes upward slightly (i.e., toward your forehead) so that you feel a mild eye strain, and then stare at a spot while keeping your eyes in that position. Do not let your gaze drift from that spot [pause for one breath]. Now when you inhale, make your stomach rise as much as you can. This is done by letting your stomach puff out as you breathe inward. It will feel as though you are breathing air into your stomach [pause for three breaths].

"Now take in an additional five deep abdominal breaths [pause for one breath]. Inhale the fifth breath extra deep, and while holding it, count backwards mentally, '5-4-3-2-1.' When you get down to '1,' exhale and close your eyes at the same time [pause for three breaths].

"Let your eyes feel relaxed, calm, perhaps tired, perhaps fatigued [pause for one breath]. Your eyes and body feel heavy, warm, tranquil [pause for one breath]. Your mind is calm, yet alert; relaxed, yet focused [pause for one breath]. You can focus more clearly now, focus more clearly on hearing your voice, focus more clearly on hearing and absorbing the content, hearing and absorbing the content of your recording—of this recording [pause for two breaths].

"Your mind can dream, and dream in detail [pause for one breath]. It goes where you ask it to go [pause for one breath]. A day off from school, free to go where you ask it to go [pause for one breath]. Imagine [pause for one breath].

"You've planned a hike, a hike up a mysterious mountain. You don't know what you'll find there [pause for one breath]. You don't know what to expect [pause for one breath]. You don't know how much positive effect it will have on you [pause for one breath]. And you realize you don't need to know [pause for one breath]. There are a lot of things you don't know before we get there [pause for one breath].

"You begin your hike, your journey, by entering a beautiful forest. The well-worn path has obviously been used by many before, but each person finds something unique along the way [pause for one breath]. They don't always know what they've found either, until later, sometimes much later, until after they have forgotten about what they didn't know they had found in the first place [pause for one breath]. Just go deeper, and enjoy the splendor of this sanctuary [pause for two breaths].

"See the path, made from nature's own hands—fallen leaves, small branches, moist dirt, green vegetation [pause for one breath]. The dense trees on either side of you stand tall, stand tall, and seem to intertwine near the top edges, leaving little light shining on the path—only certain segments where the light shines through clearly, where the light shines on the path [pause for one breath]. Smell the air, the cool, crisp, fresh, outdoor scent, the smell of foliage, the smell of humid air, the smell of a forest [pause for one breath]. Feel the gentle moisture on your skin [pause for one breath]. See the squirrels, the chipmunks, the birds—hear the sounds of birds, chirping, singing, celebrating—feel their joy, their freedom, their contentment [pause for one breath]. They seem to accept themselves as they are, you accept them as they are [pause for two breaths].

"Each bird is unique, yet is a part of a whole [pause for one breath]. You are loving both parts—loving that which is unique, and loving that which is part of the universal connection [pause for one breath]. If words could be sung by such tiny creatures, your mind wonders what those words might be [pause for one breath]. 'Breathe peace into your heart, and tranquility into your soul'—are these the words they sing? [pause for one breath] 'Be yourself, and love yourself' [pause for one breath]. Have I heard these words before? Maybe the birds are just singing, 'Have a safe journey, and don't forget what's really important in life' [pause for two breaths].

"Regardless of the content of their message, it is hard to understand, so you move on, farther along, till you reach a higher place where the forest ends and a meadow begin [pause for one breath]. Can you remember the last time you walked through a meadow? This one is more beautiful than the one you remember [pause for one breath]. As you enter the meadow, you take off your shoes and socks, and feel the dampness of moist grasses under your feet [pause for one breath]. You feel so contented, so privileged, so happy [pause for one breath]. You feel that so many of the things that had affected you, are now affecting you in more positive ways now [pause for one breath]. From every experience there is something you can learn, something you can learn from, something you can grow from, something that helps you grow [pause for one breath]. You are not perfect, and you know that every mistake is simply a failed experiment [pause for two breaths]. Life is full of experiments, and each one contains new learning, and offers a new growth opportunity [pause for one breath]. Life is full of opportunities [pause for two breaths].

"You continue to climb and move on, farther along, till you reach a higher place where the meadow ends and rocky surfaces begin. Still, the path is clear, and safe, and the incline is gradual, yet steady [pause for one breath]. A few more steps, and you see that the destination is before you [pause for one breath]. Ahead, steam is rising from a small cavity in the rock [pause for one breath]. You get closer, and you feel the warmth rising from your bare feet to your legs to your torso, your arms, and your face [pause for one breath]. It's a natural hot spring, and its call is irresistible [pause for one breath]. You remove your clothes, slowly ease yourself into the hot clear pool, and sit on a comfortable rock [pause for one breath]. Most of your body is surrounded by the warm water [pause for one breath]. Feel the water on your skin, and smell the soothing minerals it contains [pause for one breath]. As the steam rises, imagine that it is washing away all of your thoughts, all of your concerns [pause for one breath]. All that is left is perfect calmness, total peacefulness, complete serenity [pause for one breath]. Keep enjoying this state for as long as you want, especially while you listen to the last few minutes of this recording [pause for three breaths].

"The more times that you listen to this recording, the deeper your conditioning for self-hypnosis will be [pause for one breath]. This means you will enter self-hypnosis more quickly, you will create greater depth in self-hypnosis, and you will find enhanced benefits when using self-hypnosis to create changes within yourself [pause for two breaths].

"With practice, you will be able to shorten the induction of self-hypnosis to two steps, and be able to do this without listening to this recording. Don't do this now, but whenever you wish to place yourself into self-hypnosis in the future, do the following. First, with your eyes open, stare at a particular spot directly in front of your line of vision. Do not let your gaze drift from that spot [pause for one breath]. Second, take in five deep abdominal breaths. As you exhale the final deep breath, close your eyes at the same time. As you do this, you will drop into a deep state of self-hypnosis [pause for two breaths]. After you have listened to this recording enough times so that you respond to it by becoming deeply relaxed, try this abbreviated induction on your own. If you then respond to the abbreviated induction with good results, great. If not, either continue listening to this recording, or use the basic induction method as outlined in Appendix 2 [pause for two breaths].

"You are now at the end of Major Script #1, 'The Basics of Self-Hypnosis.' You may wish to continue enjoying this relaxed state for a while longer. Whenever you are ready to end this experience, first silently tell yourself that you will count to five and that at the count of five, you will come out of self-hypnosis feeling refreshed, relaxed, and confident. Then awaken yourself by counting to five mentally, and say, 'AWAKE' to yourself. Then open your eyes."

Appendix Four

Major Script #2: "Grade Power: Unlocking the Keys"

Major Script #2 is a compilation of the individual scripts found in Chapters 4 through 12. Each script is labeled here (e.g., *Belief in Yourself*) so that you can decide to exclude any of the segments that do not apply to you. For example, if you do not have a problem with *exam anxiety*, you might choose to delete this section from your recorded script. Now let's begin:

"Get comfortable, preferably lying down with your arms and legs uncrossed. Now contract all of your muscles simultaneously, and hold the tension [pause for seven breaths]. Now relax your muscles, and notice the contrast between muscle tension and relaxation [pause for four breaths]. Now contract all of your muscles simultaneously again, and hold the tension [pause for seven breaths]. Now relax your muscles, and notice the contrast once more [pause for four breaths].

"With your eyes open, roll your eyes upward slightly (i.e., toward your forehead) so that you feel a mild eye strain, and then stare at a spot while keeping your eyes in that posision. Do not let your gaze drift from that spot. Take five deep abdominal breaths [pause for two breaths]. Inhale the fifth breath extra deep, and while holding it, count backwards mentally, '5-4-3-2-1.' When you get down to '1,' exhale and close your eyes at the same time [pause for two breaths]."

Belief in Yourself
"Every day you find yourself becoming mentally healthier and stronger [pause for one breath]. You feel increasingly positive about who you are and the person you are becoming [pause for one breath]. You are letting go of perfectionistic tendencies and replacing these with a desire to be competent [pause for one breath]. This means you forgive yourself when you make mistakes, but you also learn from them so as to reduce the probability of making the same mistakes again [pause for twobreaths].

"As you develop greater competence, you also become increasingly self-confident [pause for 1 breath]. Your self-confidence steadily improves [pause for one breath]. You look forward to learning new skills and having new experiences [pause for one breath]. While you begin learning something new, you maintain a good feeling about your capability [pause for one breath]. Learning something new takes time and no one, especially yourself, expects you will be competent from the very beginning [pause for one breath]. You are a reasonable person, and you are reasonable with yourself [pause for two breaths].

"In every way each day, you become more of who you are, and less of who others are or who others want you to be [pause for one breath]. This is your life, and you need to find your own path—a road that will take you where you want to go [pause for two breaths]."

Passion
"You are motivated to know yourself more fully [pause for one breath]. You embrace the uniqueness that makes you who you are, and coming to know your likes and dislikes feels gratifying [pause for one breath]. Knowing that you don't need to like

everything or everybody is, in fact, liberating [pause for one breath]. Becoming your own person allows you to love the things and the people that really matter [pause for one breath]. You know that you will make a difference in this life—your impact will be felt [pause for one breath]. Underlying the difference you will make is great passion toward important life goals [pause for 1 breath]. Increasingly you find yourself becoming a passionate individual, a person who strives toward your own commitments and beliefs [pause for two breaths].

"Your goals are becoming ever more crystallized and more real [pause for one breath]. The more you focus on them, the more important they become to you [pause for one breath]. You deserve to succeed in school and in life [pause for one breath]. This is, after all, your life, and no one can achieve what is important to you other than yourself [pause for one breath]. You are continually coming to better terms with your priorities, and acting on them accordingly [pause for two breaths].

"Your most important goals take on deep and personal meaning [pause for one breath]. They may not have meaning to other people, and that is fine [pause for one breath]. It is enough that your goals serve your purposes in life [pause for one breath]. The more you focus on any particular goal, the more it becomes realized [pause for one breath]. Your passion toward your important goals sustains you during the times of dedicated effort [pause for one breath]. Nothing important ever occurred to anyone without dedication and perspiration [pause for one breath]. You are up for the fight—you are a passionate individual [pause for two breaths]."

Persistence

"You are becoming increasingly motivated toward important life goals [pause for one breath]. As you focus your energies on your goals, you develop increased competence in what you are doing, and this in turn increases your motivation as well [pause for one breath]. Regardless of how you feel, however, you persist in working toward the things that matter most to you [pause for one breath].

You prefer to get down to work early on projects, and it makes you feel good about yourself to do so [pause for two breaths].

"You are developing a clearer sense of your priorities in life and at school [pause for one breath]. Consequently, you work on assignments and goals [pause for one breath]. When you perceive that an assignment or goal is going to be difficult, time-consuming, or unpleasant, you break it down into manageable steps, and you reward yourself for getting each step accomplished [pause for two breaths].

"There is no better time than now to succeed in life and at school [pause for one breath]. This means you are persistent in your efforts, even when adversity tries to hold you back [pause for one breath]. Setbacks may slow you down from time to time, but you are like a bulldozer when it comes to getting the job done [pause for one breath]. You have the stamina to keep pushing forward toward achieving the goals you have set for yourself [pause for one breath]. You are ready to get down to work [pause for one breath]. Your determination is impenetrable [pause for one breath]. Like an ever-ready battery, you keep going [pause for one breath] and going [pause for one breath] and going [pause for two breaths]."

Balance

"You are striving to find a healthy balance in your life. You are committed to spending time focused on the five domains of life: school and/or work, leisure and recreation, social, physical, and spiritual. You know that school is demanding, and when you are working hard, you know that you also need to take care of your physical needs. No wonder you feel a strong desire to get adequate exercise, sufficient sleep, proper diet, and enough rest and relaxation [pause for two breaths].

"When faced with too many commitments or obligations, you prioritize these and let go or suspend temporarily the ones of lesser importance [pause for one breath]. You know that you cannot do everything at once, and you are forgiving of yourself when you need to put some things off for a time [pause for 1 breath].

When the load is too great, you are okay with saying 'no' to people's demands [pause for two breaths].

"You strive to create moderation with all things that affect your health [pause for one breath]. You are aware of what you are doing that is good for you, and you are aware of what you are doing that is not [pause for one breath]. Because you love yourself deeply, you take the necessary steps to let go or at least minimize unhealthy activities [pause for one breath]. This is your body, and you are committed to looking after it [pause for two breaths]."

Learning and Studying

"Your concentration for reading and studying is constantly improving [pause for one breath]. When you sit down to read or study, you can concentrate for longer periods of time [pause for one breath]. For whatever reason, you are becoming more focused and more interested in what you are learning about [pause for one breath]. Your mind is clear and it works efficiently [pause for two breaths].

"Your memory is also steadily improving [pause for one breath]. Your ability to learn new information is getting better and better [pause for one breath]. Because of your improved study methods, you can easily recall information whenever you want to [pause for one breath]. Your mind works like a high-speed computer [pause for one breath]—you retain that which you input, and you remember that which is needed for output [pause for two breaths].

"You find it interesting how your motivation to study is growing [pause for one breath]. Your goals are important to you, and achieving good or exceptional grades in school will help you immensely [pause for one breath]. Part of the exercise is learning to be well disciplined in life, so you know that all of the studying is serving you well [pause for one breath]. You feel confident in your ability to learn [pause for one breath]. You review your material periodically, reciting either out loud or silently that which you have learned [pause for two breaths]."

Exam Anxiety

"You are well prepared for exams and you feel confident in your ability [pause for one breath]. Once you take your seat in the room where you will be writing the exam, you feel a sense of belonging in that seat and this feeling comforts you [pause for one breath]. You become cool, calm, and collected when you write exams [pause for one breath]. The excitement you feel is only about feeling pumped for the challenge you are about to face [pause for two breaths].

"You can accept whatever the result of your performance will be because you are not perfect [pause for one breath]. Furthermore, you are neither the one who decides what the test will look like nor the one who determines its difficulty level [pause for one breath]. That is why you focus your time and energy on learning and accept that you do not fully control the outcome [pause for one breath]. If you were a surgeon, for example, you would only have control over your knowledge and your performance [pause for one breath]. The outcome is not fully within your control [pause for one breath]. The patient might not improve as a result of the surgery, and something unforeseen could occur [pause for one breath]. Similarly, you only control your learning and your performance, and you can fully accept the outcome, whatever it looks like [pause for two breaths].

"If you need to become more relaxed during an exam, you can simply put your pen or pencil down for a minute, and simultaneously contract all of your muscles [pause for one breath]. Alternatively, you can tilt your eyes back slightly, take five deep abdominal breaths, and then breathe out and close your eyes at the same time [pause for one breath]. Once done, you can tell yourself the messages you need to hear, such as 'I am regaining my composure and becoming totally focused on this exam. I am here to do my best, and that is what I will do right now' [pause for two breaths].

"If you come to a question that you can't immediately answer, tell yourself, 'When I return to this question, I will remember the answer to it' [pause for one breath]. Then move on to the next question. This will act like a post-hypnotic suggestion and will increase the likelihood that the answer will return [pause for onr breath]. If you didn't study the answer to a question, give yourself this suggestion instead, 'I don't know the answer to this question, but I do know most of this material' [pause for one breath]. This suggestion will keep you motivated with momentum [pause for two breaths]."

Writer's Block

"Your thinking is becoming clearer, and this results in better writing [pause for one breath]. Because you can talk, this means you can write [pause for one breath]. You can now feel confident in your ability to write because with proper editing, you will be writing well [pause for one breath]. You are also motivated to learn more about how to improve your writing [pause for two breaths].

"If you have a writing project to do for which you have no choice on the topic, you develop the necessary discipline to work on it and complete it in a timely manner [pause for one breath]. If necessary, you provide yourself with rewards for getting segments of the project completed [pause for one breath]. If you are given the choice of a topic to write about, you select one about which you feel passionate [pause for one breath]. You will find that your subconscious mind helps you in various ways to come up with a good topic [pause for one breath]. It might happen that a great idea is given to you in a dream, or upon waking [pause for one breath]. It may just be that an idea will pop into your head as you go about your daily routines [pause for one breath]. For these reasons, it is always a good idea to carry around a notepad and a pen with you at all times when you are searching for a topic [pause for two breaths].

"When you need to take a break from writing, you get some exercise or switch to another project for a while [pause for one breath]. Afterwards, you soon regain the momentum needed to return to writing [pause for one breath]. The writing project will get done [pause for one breath]. Your writing doesn't need to be perfect, and neither do you. Instead, you strive to become a competent individual [pause for two breaths]."

Speech Anxiety

"Whenever you are to give a speech or presentation, you prepare extensively for it [pause for one breath]. You learn your material well so that the content is mostly committed to memory [pause for one breath]. You also practice your speech several times, both out loud and in your imagination [pause for one breath]. You remember to use relaxation exercises, such as abdominal breathing, to help you become comfortable before getting up to give your presentation [pause for two breaths].

"Rather than having your speech written out word for word, you instead have a key-word outline in front of you [pause for one breath]. You are amazed that although you feel some excitement before giving your talk, you soon become cool, calm, and collected in front of your audience [pause for one breath]. Your passion also comes through as you find ways to modulate your voice dynamics to enhance interest [pause for two breaths].

"You are finding that it is okay to become the center of attention when you give a talk [pause for one breath]. Although people's eyes are focused on you, they are mostly focused on what you have to say [pause for one breath]. You speak with confidence and authority—you find your voice, and your voice is strong and full of impact [pause for one breath]. You have something to say, and you want to say it when given the opportunity [pause for one breath]. With practice, you find that you begin to enjoy giving speeches and presentations [pause for two breaths]."

Career Exploration

"Finding a suitable career choice is one of the most important decisions you will make in your life [pause for one breath]. You recognize that there is no one perfect career choice, but there are several good choices that you need to discover [pause for one breath]. It is imperative that you spend sufficient time on this task so that you come up with an appropriate career plan [pause for one breath]. Consequently, you are motivated to take the necessary steps to learn more about yourself and your interests [pause for one breath]. You also feel motivated to take the necessary steps to learn more about the world of work and about career opportunities [pause for two breaths].

"Often your mind takes you to thinking about your career options [pause for one breath]. Sometimes you find yourself fantasizing about working in different careers [pause for one breath]. Your dreams sometimes reveal interesting career choices to you, and you remember them in the morning so that you can write them down [pause for one breath]. Both your conscious and subconscious minds are working together as a team to help you with this goal [pause for two breaths].

"Not only do you use imagery to help you to consider different career alternatives, but you also use it to prepare for job interviews [pause for one breath]. You envisage yourself in the job interview situation itself, visualizing as fully as possible how composed and confident you feel [pause for one breath]. You also anticipate questions that might be asked of you, and how you will respond to these questions [pause for one breath]. You include the nonverbal aspects as well, such as having a steady calm voice, and having appropriate voice volume, voice tone, facial expressions, and body posture [pause for two breaths]."

Awakening Instructions

"When you are ready to leave self-hypnosis, first silently tell yourself that you will count to five and that at the count of five, you will come out of self-hypnosis feeling refreshed, relaxed, and confident. Then awaken yourself by counting to five mentally, and say, 'AWAKE!' to yourself [pause for three breaths]. Then open your eyes."

Appendix Five

How to Use Visual Imagery in Self-Hypnosis

Visualization is like daydreaming, only it is directed by you. It is best accomplished while being relaxed. You relax deeply every night before you fall asleep. Consequently, relaxing is actually nothing new to you. There are many different ways to relax, and below I suggest the simplest way of doing so.

1. *Lie down in a comfortable place.* This place could be your couch, your bed, or on a recliner.

2. *Close your eyes.* Let yourself become calm and relaxed. If you want to relax deeply, let it happen. In a deep relaxation, you will probably not want to move at all. You might also feel heavy, warm, and tired.

3. *Begin to visualize.* As clearly as you can, imagine that which has been suggested to you in the chapter you are reading. This means to picture it in your mind's eye, similar to daydreaming about it.

4. *Create as much detail as you can.* The best visual images are detailed. If you are visualizing a burning candle, see the shape and size of the candle, picture its burning wick, imagine the flame darting about, and see the wax dripping down its sides and falling onto its holder.

5. *Allow as many of your senses into the visual image as possible.* For example, imagine hearing people talk to you or other sounds (like ocean waves), bring in the sense of smell (what does ocean air smell like? What about the smell of melting chocolate?), add color, allow the tactile to develop (in a beach scene, feel the sun's warmth upon your skin, and the sand under your feet), and even taste (such as the taste of candy floss).

That's all you need to do to derive benefit from visualization exercises. Continue to do these daily, for ten to fifteen minutes, until you are satisfied with the improvement that you have made in the given area.

Appendix Six

How to Use Verbal Suggestions and Positive Affirmations

Each chapter in Parts II and III of this book contain five suggestions that can be used as verbal suggestions, positive affirmations, or both. Below are instructions for how you use them:

▶ **Using Verbal Suggestions with Self-Hypnosis**
Use the Suggestions Contained in Parts II and III

1. Each chapter includes five verbal suggestions/affirmations. Pick one of these for use in self-hypnosis.

2. Read the suggestion to yourself five times before entering self-hypnosis. The suggestion should be read slowly, meaningfully, and reflectively so that it becomes the most important thought entering your mind.

3. Place yourself into self-hypnosis using the basic induction found in Appendix 2 and remain there for at least three or four minutes.

4. During these three or four minutes (or longer), you will find that the words in the suggestion begin to enter your mind in an automatic or semi-automatic fashion, although not necessarily in

their correct sequence. If the words are not forthcoming on their own, use as little effort as possible to bring the key words of the suggestion into your mind.

5. Awaken yourself in the usual manner.

Use Your Own Suggestions

In each chapter, there is room for you to write your own suggestions for later use as verbal suggestions, positive affirmations, or both. Below are instructions for how you use them:

1. Write positively worded suggestions in the book or on a separate sheet of paper. Pick one of these for use in self-hypnosis. Each suggestion should be a one-sentence statement that conveys the intent of your goal. For example, if you wanted to become a calmer individual, you should *not* use the suggestion, *"I will try to become less* tense *each day"* for two reasons. First, the word *try* implies the possibility of failure to your subconscious mind, and secondly the word *tense* may actually increase your tension. Instead, find a more positive word that means its direct opposite. For example, a positive suggestion is, *"I will become* calmer *each day."* The word *calm* suggests the desired outcome.

2. Read the suggestion to yourself five times before entering self-hypnosis. The suggestion should be read slowly, meaningfully, and reflectively so that it becomes the most important thought entering your mind.

3. Place yourself into self-hypnosis using the basic induction found in Appendix 2 and remain there for at least three or four minutes.

4. During this three or four minutes (or longer), you will find that the words in the suggestion begin to enter your mind in an automatic or semi-automatic fashion, although not necessarily in their correct sequence. If the words are not forthcoming on their own, use as little effort as possible to bring the key words of your suggestion into your mind.

5. Awaken yourself in the usual manner.

▶ Using Positive Affirmations

The suggestions contained in each chapter, or the ones you write yourself, can be used as positive affirmations. An affirmation is like a suggestion, a message you give to yourself repeatedly. The intent is that, over time, the affirmation will become internalized, meaning that you begin to believe it. If you haven't read the section above called, *Using Your Own Suggestions*, review now the first point that explains how to write a positively-worded suggestion/affirmation.

1. Re-write or type the positively-worded affirmations into large print on a single sheet of paper, and keep this list by your bed.

2. Then read the list to yourself five times before you go to sleep, and five times when you wake up. Each time you read it, concentrate on it and think about what it means to you.

3. Feel free to add in visual images that also contain the theme(s) of the affirmations.

4. The entire exercise of using affirmations need take only two or three minutes.

Appendix Seven

Progressive Muscle Relaxation Script

Progressive Muscle Relaxation teaches you how to physically relax every major muscle group in your body. By practicing this technique, you will learn how to turn a tight muscle into a relaxed muscle at will. The following script was prepared by Gregory E. Harris, and it is included here with his permission. Remember that if you have a medical condition that precludes you from doing any of the specific muscle contraction exercises contained in this script, avoid doing them.

Whenever you want to listen to your tape, first find a comfortable spot on a well-supported chair, a couch, or a bed. You want your entire body to feel comfortable. Record the entire script below using the instructions found in Appendix 1.

"Take a deep breath from your diaphragm, hold it for a few seconds, and then allow it to flow out from your mouth [pause for two breaths]. Notice the quiet and peacefulness in your relaxation place [pause for one breath]. Take a few more deep breaths just like the one before and allow yourself to notice whatever is coming to your mind [pause for one breath]. At this point you may be already starting to feel some relaxation happening in your body [pause for one breath]. That's okay; this will become a more and more natural feeling as you practice this relaxation exercise [pause for two breaths].

"Squeeze your right hand into a tight fist and feel the tension and pressure in your hand and forearm [pause for three breaths]. Maintain this tension for about five seconds and notice how it feels, focusing on the tension and pressure [pause for three breaths]. Feel it all the way up your arm [pause for one breath]. Now just let it relax [pause for one breath]. Just let your arm go limp [pause for one breath]. Notice the relaxed feeling that happens when you just let the tension go [pause for one breath]. Feel the relaxed feeling [pause for one breath].

"Now tense your right hand again, and feel the tension [pause for three breaths]. Focus on the tension and how it makes you feel [pause for one breath]. Pay attention to the pressure [pause for one breath]. Now let it relax [pause for one breath]. Notice the difference it makes to relax [pause for one breath]. Feel the difference when you relax [pause for one breath]. Just notice the relaxation feeling in your hand and forearm [pause for one breath].

"Now flex your right bicep muscle [pause for three breaths]. Feel the tension and pressure in your muscle [pause for one breath]. Hold this tension for about five seconds and just feel the tension [pause for one breath]. Now let it relax [pause for one breath]. Let it just feel relaxed [pause for one breath]. Notice the difference between the relaxation and tension [pause for one breath]. Focus on this difference, and feel the feeling of relaxation [pause for one breath]. Feel it in your body [pause for 1 breath].

"Flex your right bicep again, and notice how it feels [pause for three breaths]. Pay attention to this feeling of tension and pressure [pause for one breath]. Just feel the tension [pause for one breath]. Then, just allow it to release [pause for one breath]. Feel the difference between the relaxation and the tension [pause for one breath]. Just notice the relaxed feeling [pause for one breath]. Just enjoy that calm, relaxed feeling in your body [pause for 1 breath].

"When you are ready, squeeze your left hand into a tight fist [pause for three breaths]. Hold this tight for about five seconds and notice the tension and pressure in your hand and forearm [pause for one breath]. Experience the tension and pressure [pause for one breath]. Now just let that fist go and fall into a relaxed position [pause for one breath]. Just feel the relaxing difference [pause for one breath]. Notice how you can control the relaxation and tension [pause for one breath]. Just feel the relaxation in your hand and forearm [pause for one breath].

"Now squeeze your left hand again [pause for three breaths]. Notice the tension and pressure in your hand and forearm [pause for one breath]. Focus on the tension [pause for one breath]. Now let it relax once again [pause for one breath]. Feel free to just focus on how relaxed and limp your hand and forearm feel [pause for one breath]. Just notice the relaxed feeling in your body [pause for one breath]. Notice the differences between relaxation and tension, and how good it feels to be relaxed [pause for one breath]."

Continue this script, changing only the body part that is focused on. Substitute tensing your left bicep, wrinkling your forehead, tensing your cheeks with a large smile, and tightening your jaw. Each action should be enacted twice, just as above.

Continue with some encouragement:

"You have been doing a very good job of becoming relaxed [pause for one breath]. You notice the changes in your body from when you first started this relaxation exercise [pause for one breath]. You may notice a relaxing feeling of being at peace throughout all those parts of your body that you have already relaxed [pause for one breath]. It can be useful to review those parts to remind yourself how relaxed you really are and also to give yourself the chance to relax those parts even more deeply [pause for one breath]. As you read through the list, feel free to remember the feeling of relaxation in each part of your body [pause for one breath]. If there is a part that you feel could be even more relaxed, just repeat the relaxation steps that you already enacted [pause for one breath]. Just go at your own pace [pause for one breath]. Take all the time you need [pause for one breath].

"Focus on your right hand and forearm, feel how relaxed they are [pause for one breath]. Notice the relaxing feeling in your right bicep [pause for one breath]. Take some time to enjoy that feeling [pause for one breath]. Notice the relaxation in your left hand and forearm [pause for one breath]. Feel the relaxation in your left bicep [pause for one breath]. This feeling of relaxation goes all the way into your head and face [pause for one breath], with nice, warm feelings into your forehead and cheeks [pause for one breath], and down into your jawbones [pause for one breath]. Just feel this warm relaxation feeling for a few seconds [pause for one breath].

"When you are ready, tense your shoulders and upper back…"

Continue your script, tensing your shoulders and upper back again, then tense your stomach muscles and lower back again, and again tense your right thigh and calf. Point your toes up in the air, and tense your right foot again. Next, tense your left thigh and calf, put your toes back in the air, and tense your left foot again.

"You are still doing a great job of relaxing [pause for one breath]. You have relaxed your entire body [pause for one breath]. Part of learning to become deeply relaxed is learning to notice the difference between tension and relaxation [pause for one breath]. You can learn to recognize when your body is feeling tense and then how to take control and relax—like you have done here today [pause for one breath]. The more you practice the more control you will have [pause for one breath].

"It is important to remember all of the relaxing that you have done here today so you can see how relaxed you are [pause for one breath]. As you read through all of the parts of your body that you have relaxed, feel free to notice just how relaxed they are feeling [pause for one breath]. If you think something could be more relaxed, just spent some time reviewing the relaxation steps you have already done, and use them for that part of your body [pause for one breath].

"Just go at your own pace [pause for one breath]. Take all the time you need [pause for one breath]. Focus on your right hand and forearm, feel how relaxed they are [pause for one breath]. Notice the relaxed feeling in your right bicep [pause for one breath]. Take some time to enjoy that feeling [pause for one breath]. Notice the relaxation in your left hand and forearm [pause for one breath]. Feel the relaxation in your left bicep [pause for one breath]. This relaxation feeling goes all the way into your head and face [pause for one breath]. Feel the nice warm feelings into your forehead and cheeks [pause for one breath]. Down into your jawbones [pause for one breath]. Just feel this warm feeling of relxation for a few seconds [pause for one breath].

"Notice the feelings of deep relaxation in your shoulders and upper back [pause for one breath]. Feeling warm and relaxed [pause for one breath]. Take a deep breath, and notice how you are feeling [pause for one breath]. Notice how the relaxed feeling extends through your chest [pause for one breath], and down into your stomach and lower back [pause for one breath]. Feel how it moves into your legs [pause for one breath]. The relaxation goes through your thighs and into your calves [pause for one breath]. Feel it go all the way into your feet [pause for one breath]. Just sit for as long as you like, and enjoy this feeling of deep relaxation [pause for one breath].

"It is important for you to know that even when you stop this relaxation exercise you can still allow yourself to continue feeling deeply relaxed [pause for one breath]. You can practice this exercise as often as you like, wherever you like [pause for one breath]. One way that can help you to reorientate yourself back into your room is by counting [pause for one breath]. You can count forward from one to five [pause for one breath]. This will give you time to wake up and feel refreshed [pause for one breath]. With each number you say, you can feel more and more relaxed and awake [pause for one breath]. Take your time and go at your own speed [pause for one breath]. One [pause for one breath], feeling deeply relaxed [pause for one breath]. Two [pause for one breath], feeling relaxed and refreshed [pause for 1 breath]. Three [pause for one breath], starting to feel more awake [pause for one breath]. Four [pause for one breath], noticing the sounds more clearly in your relaxation place [pause for one breath]. Five [pause for one breath], waking up and feeling refreshed and awake."

Appendix Eight

Your Plan for Change

1. Goal Setting
a) What is the most important change that I wish to make in myself? (For multiple goals, complete one form for each important change desired.)

b) What are my reasons for wanting to make this change?

c) If I change, how would I:
Behave differently?
Think differently?
Feel differently?

2. Base Rates
Regarding the changes that you would like to make in question (c) above, how would you rate your present ability to behave, think, and feel in the desired manner? Use the following abbreviations for this question:
VD = very difficult
D = difficult

S = so-so
E = easy
VE = very easy

	Behave	Think	Feel
The ease with which I do this now is			
The frequency with which I do this now is			
The quality of this is now			

3. Treatment Plan

a) In what ways can I realize this goal using hypnosis?

b) Besides hypnosis, what other strategies will assist me in accomplishing my goal?

c) What factors may prevent or hinder me from attaining my goal?

Appendix Nine

Self-Assessment Toward Academic Success

There are many reasons why students do not do as well in school as they had hoped. Place a checkmark beside those factors that you anticipate may be a problem for you:

# Type of Concern	Is There a Self-Hypnosis Application? (specify what you intend to do)

Time Management Concerns

1 Poor time management skills.

2 Procrastination.

3 Too many other commitments
____(a) part-time or full-time job
____(b) family responsibilities
____(c) other

4 Insufficient time spent with assignments.

Academic Concerns

5 Insufficient academic background (i.e., you were not adequately prepared).

6 Inappropriate course selection (i.e., you took courses that you did not want, need or like).

7 Difficulties in the area of:

____(a) reading skills

____(b) writing skills

____(c) math skills

____(d) memorization

____(e) exam anxiety

____(f) notetaking

____(g) inefficient study strategies

____(h) concentration

Other Concerns

8 Career uncertainty.

9 Financial difficulties.

10 Lack of motivation, boredom, or apathy.

11 Low energy level.

12 Difficulties in the area of:

____(a) regular exercise

____(b) healthy diet

____(c) sleep

____(d) social/recreational activities

____(e) excessive use of drugs/alcohol

____(f) problem behaviors

13 Lack of readiness or desire to be a student.

14 Lack of commitment to school.

15 Lack of assertiveness.

16 Experienced a recent crisis.

17 Emotional difficulties (i.e., depression, anxiety).

18 Difficulties with relationships.

20 Self-defeating attitudes/beliefs (i.e., you view things negatively, especially yourself and your own capabilities).

21 Physical Illness.

22 Home problems.

23 Learning disability.

24 Other problem not covered by this inventory (specify):

References

Arons, H., & Bubeck, M. F. H. 1971. *The Handbook of Professional Hypnosis*. New Jersey: Power Publishers.

Bancroft, W. J. 1976. Suggestology and suggestopedia: The theory of the Lozanov method. *Journal of Suggestive-Accelerative Learning and Teaching*, 1(3), 187–216.

Brown, D., Scheeflin, A. W., & Hammond, D. C. 1998. *Memory, Trauma Treatment, and the Law*. New York: Norton.

Canadian Institute for Health Information. 1999. *Statistical Report on the Health of Canadians*. Retrieved May 26, 2004 from http://secure.cihi.ca/cihiweb/dispPage.jsp?cw_page=repor ts_statistical _e

Cohen, H. A. 1982. The Use of Clinical Hypnosis in a College Counseling Center. (Paper presented at the Annual Convention of the American Personnel and Guidance Association—Detroit, MI, March 17–20, 1982). EDRS (ED222804).

Cohen, L. R. (n.d.) *Advice from the Prolific*. Retrieved May 31, 2004 from http://www.sff.net/people/LisaRC/advice.htm

Counseling Center for Human Development at the University of South Florida. (n.d.) *Speech Anxiety*. Retrieved June 3, 2004 from http://isis.fastmail.usf.edu/counsel/self-hlp/speech.htm

Craig, J. P. (n.d.) *Rhetoric 10:02:24 Online Resources*. Retrieved June 3, 2004 from http://www.uiowa.edu/~c100298/anxiety.html

Craik, F. I. M., & Lockhart, R. S. 1972. "Levels of Processing: A Framework for Memory Research." *Journal of Verbal Learning and Verbal Behavior, 11,* 671–684.

Edmonston, W.E. 1977. "Neutral Hypnosis as Relaxation." *American Journal of Clinical Hypnosis,* 20(1), 69-75.

Genuit, D.W. 1994. *Altered States Hypnosis and Healers.* Retrieved June 19, 2004 from http://earthkeeper.freeservers.com/cgi_bin/ad/inline?page=altered+genuit.htm&Rtime=9140.

Gerler, E. R., Jr. 1980. "Mental Imagery in Multimodal Career Education." *Vocational Guidance Quarterly, 28,* 306-312.

Hartland, J. 1971. *Medical and Dental Hypnosis and its Clinical Applications.* London: Bailliere Tindall.

Hill, N. 1960. *Think and Grow Rich.* New York: Ballantine Books.

Johnson, S. 1997. *Taking the Anxiety out of Taking Tests: A Step-by-Step Guide.* Oakland, CA: Harbinger.

Kihlstrom, J. F., & Barnhardt, T. M. 1993. "The Self-Regulation of Memory: For Better and for Worse, With and Without Hypnosis." In D. M. Wegner, J. W. Pennebaker, et al. (Eds.), *Handbook of Mental Control* (pp. 88–125). Englewood Cliffs, NJ: Prentice-Hall.

Merriam-Webster's Collegiate Dictionary (11th ed.). 2003. Springfield, MA: Merriam-Webster.

Morgan, J. I., & Skovholt, T. M. 1977. "Using Inner Experience: Fantasy and Daydreams in Career Counseling." *Journal of Counseling Psychology, 24,* 391–397.

Moss, R. L., & Young, R. B. 1995. "Perceptions About the Academic and Social Integration of Underprepared Students in an Urban Community College." *Community College Review, 22*(4), 47–61.

Napier, N. J. 1990. *Recreating Yourself: Building Self-Esteem Through Imaging and Self-Hypnosis.* New York: Norton.

Owen, D., & Wilson, J. 1980. "Cowboys and Butterflies: Creative Uses of Spontaneous Fantasy in Career Counseling." *School Counselor, 28,* 119–125.

Prochaska, J. O., Norcross, J. C., & Diclemente, C. C. 1994. *Changing for Good: A Revolutionary Six-Stage Program.*

Raikov, V. L. (1976). "The Possibility of Creativity in the Active Stage of Hypnosis." *International Journal of Clinical & Experimental Hypnosis, 24,* 258–268.

Reupert, A., & Maybery, D. 2000. "Hypnosis in a Case of Vocational Counselling." *Australian Journal of Clinical and Experimental Hypnosis, 28,* 74–81.

Saltzman, J. 1993. *If You Can Talk, You Can Write.* New York: Warner.

Sarnoff, D., & Remer, P. 1982. "The Effects of Guided Imagery on the Generation of Career Alternatives." *Journal of Vocational Behavior, 21,* 299–308.

Skovholt, T. M., Morgan, J. I., & Negron-Cunningham, H. 1989. "Mental Imagery in Career Counseling and Life Planning: A Review of Research and Intervention Methods." *Journal of Counseling & Development, 67,* 287–292.

Strunk, W., & White, E. B. 2000. *The Elements of Style* (4th ed.). Toronto: Allyn & Bacon.

Stanton, H. E. 1988. "Improving Examination Performance Through the Clenched Fist Technique." *Contemporary Educational Psychology, 13*, 309–315.

Thomas, C. (n.d.) *Conquering Speech Anxiety*. Retrieved June 3, 2004 from http://www.roxbury.net/cps6chape.pdf

University of Texas at Austin Counseling & Mental Health Center. 1999. *Better Self-Esteem*. Retrieved May 10, 2004 from http://www.utexas.edu/student/cmhc/booklets/selfesteem/selfest.html

Waddell, M. L., Esch, R. M., & Walker, R. R. 1993. *The Art of Styling Sentences: 20 Patterns for Success*. Hauppauge, NY: Barrons Educational Series.

Weiten, W., & Lloyd, M. A. 2003. *Psychology Applied to Modern Life* (7th ed.). Toronto: Nelson Thomson Learning.

Welcome to the Wonderful World of Baroque Music. (n.d.) Retrieved May 23, 2004 from http://www.baroquemusic.org

Wilson, W. C., & Eddy, J. 1982. "Guided Imagery in Career Awareness." *Rehabilitation Counseling Bulletin, 25*, 291–295.

Ziegenfuss, W. B. 1962. "Hypnosis: A Tool for Education." *Education, 82*, 505–507.

Index